I0743695

The Mad Man on First Street

and

Other Short Stories

By David Chasumba

First published in Great Britain in 2022 by:

Carnelian Heart Publishing Ltd

Suite A

82 James Carter Road Mildenhall

Suffolk IP28 7DE UK

www.carnelianheartpublishing.co.uk

Paperback ISBN 978-1-914287-32-9

Hardback ISBN 978-1-914287-33-6

A CIP catalogue record for this book is available from the British Library.

This collection of short stories is entirely a work of fiction. The names, characters and incidents portrayed in it are the work of the author's imagination. Any resemblance to actual persons, living or dead, is purely coincidental.

Editors:

Lazarus Panashe Nyagwambo

Samantha Rumbidzai Vazhure

Cover design & Interior layout:

Typeset by Carnelian Heart Publishing Ltd

Layout and formatting by DanTs Media

Table of Contents

Acknowledgements	7
An Elegy for Aunt Betty	9
The Man who had the hands of a Baboon	19
The Madman on First Street	23
Crossing the Rubicon	30
The Miniskirt March	41
A Mum Indeed	49
Baptism of Fire	58
Prisoner of Conscience	62
The Promised Land	72
The Miser and the Golden Leaf	81
Lazarus rose from the dead	87
Scars of a Tree	95
One-Way Ticket Out of Hell	106
About the author	113

For Loveness, David (jnr), Tendai Joseph, Ropafadzo and Anesu. Thanks for bringing me so much joy. I love you all dearly. For my late parents, Sainett Garamukanwa Chasumba and Bessie Dhliwayo Chasumba. I miss you every day. For the entire Chasumba family, Zveushe family, Mutyora family, Mugwara family, Mutyambizi family, Mudzingwa family, Mungororo family, Nhekairo family, Marashe family, Ndirigu family, Chakanyuka family, Shoko family, Mativenga family, Muramani family, Kashanu family and to many more wonderful people who know me well, including my good old friend, Stan Mukwenya.

Acknowledgements

Many thanks to the editors of different short story anthologies and online literary journals that have previously published earlier versions of my short stories.

Anthologies:

The Promised Land in *The Bundle of Joy and Other Stories from Africa* by Africa Book Club (2014)

The Man who had the hands of a Baboon in *Small Worlds anthology* by University of Brighton Literature Society (2014)

An Elegy for Aunt Betty in *Momaya Short Story Review*: *Treasure* (2015)

Baptism of Fire in *Reflections anthology* by University of Brighton Literature Society (2015)

Online Literary Journals:

The two short stories, *The Promised Land* and *The Miser and the Golden Leaf* were published on *Africa Book Club website* (2014)

Three short stories; *The Mad Man on First Street, Scars of a Tree and Lazarus rose from the dead* were published by Kalahari Review.

Competitions:

My short story, *Crossing the Rubicon*, was longlisted in the Fish Publishing Short Story Competition (2013-2014).

***

Special thanks to my editors Samantha Rumbidzai Vazhure and Panashe Nyagwambo, and Sue Moorcroft and Margaret James, my creative writing tutors at the London School of Journalism. Thanks, Jehovah.

"In all my stories and novels, no one ever escapes Louisiana. Maybe that is because my soul never left Louisiana, although my body did go to California."

Ernest J Gaines (1933-2019)

"My six words of advice to writers are: "Read, read, read, write, write, write."

Ernest J Gaines (1933- 2019)

"A myth is an old lie that people believe in. White people believe that they're better than anyone else on earth- and it's a myth."

Ernest J Gaines, *A Lesson Before Dying*

An Elegy for Aunt Betty

Dear Aunt Betty,

I was sad and shocked when I learnt you had been sectioned in St Anne's Mental Hospital under the Mental Health Act because you refused to eat food and your social worker deemed you a risk to yourself due to depression.

Immediately, I rushed to see you on that bright, sunny Friday morning. Thoughts ran around my mind in quick orbits. Why were you trying to starve yourself to death when we had talked things over and I had agreed to stand by you through the bouts of depression?

My heart thumped as I strode into the small room with a small bed and two chairs. Bright sunrays filtered in through the blue blinds.

You stood up from your bed and came forward to greet me. Your sullen face lit up like a star when you saw me.

My intestines tightened.

"Thanks, for coming, Kid Simba." You gave me a friendly, but weary smile.

I kissed, hugged and patted you on the back.

"How are you?"

"Fed up with the depression."

"I know you can beat the depression. But you need to be resilient. The matter with the house is now water under the bridge, you must now move on. I will support you all the way."

"Some days, I am fine. But on others, a dark cloud engulfs my mind and I just want to die." Tears glistened in your eyes and slowly trickled down your cheeks.

Your hair was shrivelled and grey. Deep furrows had formed on your brow, cheeks and mouth. You sat on a chair, too frail to remain standing. Your bony hands trembled in your lap.

There was a brief silence.

I cleared my throat and looked you in the eyes. "I've made plans for you to move in with me and my family in Brixton when you are discharged from here. Camilla, your social worker, agrees with the arrangement. I hope you agree to that?"

You hesitated and avoided eye contact. Your eyes stared into empty space.

"I don't wish to burden you, Kid Simba," you said, shifting your gaze to me and forcing a smile.

"You won't burden me. I want to care for you. I want to return the favour; you were there for me in those early student days when I came to study in England." Your face beamed, reminiscing.

"Does your wife agree to this arrangement?"

"Of course, Chido agrees."

I phoned Chido and you spoke to her. She was looking forward to caring for you.

"That is so kind of you. But I am not sure that is the right thing to do." You began to sob.

"Of course, it is!" I handed you some tissues.

For an hour, we chatted about my family, my work, the past and life in general. By the time I left, I was relieved to see you laugh and joke like old times. But your actions were deceiving.

On the way home, I smiled when I recounted the cold, wet autumn morning, when we first met, inside the Afro-Caribbean shop in Hastings.

When I saw you that day, I stared at you, and you stared back.

You were a slender, beautiful African woman in her early sixties with plenty of makeup and a face well-polished with face cream. You wore a tight-fitting pair of jeans and a floral blouse. You had an Afro hair style, and your perfume was loud. You were full of life.

I was a thin, lonely, underfed twenty-year-old student, struggling to adjust to the cold and wet English weather. My self-esteem was low.

"Where do you originate from, kid?" you asked me flippantly, in fluent English.

"Zimbabwe."

"I am also from Zimbabwe," you said, your face beaming. "I have lived in England for twenty-five years though." My eyebrows rose with curiosity.

"You don't look Zimbabwean. You look like an African-American." I conversed in my funny Sub-Saharan accent.

"Thanks. So, what brought you all the way to England, kid?" You were inquisitive.

"I am reading for a BA degree in English Literature at the University of Sussex."

"Good. What do you want to do after university?"

"Teach and become a writer," I declared confidently.

"That sounds interesting. You want to be the next great African writer like Chinua Achebe or Ngugi?"

"Yes." You smiled and nodded your head.

"What do you do for a living?" I asked you.

"I have been a nurse for most of my working life, and I retire in two years."

"Good luck in retirement."

We talked at length about how the cold and wet Autumn weather dampened moods, the challenge of being a non-native English speaker, the confusion of adjusting and fitting into a western lifestyle and the nostalgia for the old country.

"Would you like to come to my home on Sunday afternoon to meet my husband and have lunch? Looks like you could do with a delicious home-cooked meal, kid."

"That is fine."

"I live at number 10 London Road. Come at 2 pm sharp. We have a lot of catching up to do about the old country." You scribbled down your house number and mobile phone number.

"I will see you then. Good day."

We parted.

***

I was at your doorstep pressing the buzzer ten minutes before 2 pm on Sunday afternoon. You invited me into the neat, warm, spacious lounge with picture frames on the walls. The smell of lavender filled the room. I slumped into the luxurious leather sofa.

You introduced me to John, your husband, a short stubby white Englishman with grey hair and small blue eyes that glared at me with suspicion. Later, John relaxed. He went out for a round of golf.

With the house left to us, we spoke freely, sharing jokes in Shona and giggling like children.

"Where did you meet John?"

You smiled, recollecting. "Salisbury. Back in the day, I looked like Angela Davis. I looked like a model, with my Afro hair, high heels and miniskirts. My skin was smooth and light because I used Ambi skin lotion. John was a backpacking English tourist. It was love at first sight. The rest is, as they say, history." We laughed.

"What was it like being an interracial couple in Rhodesia?"

"At the time, interracial relationships were frowned upon by both black and white people. But John and I were mad in love. We decided to move to England, and we got married the day after we arrived."

"Wow! That was romantic."

"Life in England wasn't as bad as in war-torn Rhodesia. In this country no one minds another person's business."

You prepared *Sadza* with barbecued pork ribs, some steamy, spicy soup and spring greens cooked in peanut butter. The tongue watering food reminded me of my mother's cooked meals back in my village in Murewa.

You showed me your big photo album; one photo of you smiling with pink dyed hair, another in which you were showing off a new tattoo and nose piercing, one of you and John sunbathing on the Hastings Beach, eating ice cream at the pier and many more.

"Lovely photos."

"Thanks."

"Will you ever return to the old country?" You frowned.

You told me that your parents perished in the Rhodesian bush war when their village was bombed by the Rhodesian air force following false accusations of aiding the ZANLA freedom fighters. You could not go back to such horrific memories.

There was momentary silence.

"Zimbabwe is now independent and peaceful. You should consider visiting home or even buying a home there."

"I do not think so." You shrugged your shoulders.

We debated the meaning of the word, 'home.' You said home was the place where you hung your knickers to dry. I said that home was the place where your umbilical cord was buried in the soil with your ancestors. We agreed to disagree.

That was the beginning of our friendship.

You insisted on me calling you Aunt Betty. You preferred to call me Kid Simba, even though I was a young adult, and my full name was Simbarashe. I did not mind you calling me that. It was your banter.

I became the cousin you did not have.

After university, I moved to London to teach and began to write. We stayed connected through phone calls, letters, and visits at festive seasons.

Eventually, I got married and started a family. But I never forgot you, your friendship and warm hospitality during my hectic student days.

***

One day, you phoned me. "I have changed my mind. I want to buy a home in Zimbabwe," you said. Your voice was full of joy.

"Great! Why did you change your mind?"

"I reunited with a long-lost cousin back home. His name is Batsirai. We grew up together and we were close. He owns an estate agency, and he persuaded me to invest there."

"I am happy you saw the light. How will you finance the purchase of the house?"

"I will use my pension, topped up with a bank loan. I will use my house as collateral."

"Does John support the plan?"

"No. He opposes it. He thinks it is too risky. But I have to win him over."

"Poor John."

"Do you have any advice for me?"

"Before the purchase, verify that your cousin's estate agency is legitimate. There are bogus estate agencies in Harare. Also verify that the house has title deeds and sign the agreement of sale through a reputable law firm."

"Thanks, kid Simba." You hung up.

A week later, you phoned back. You had done your research; everything checked out and you trusted your cousin.

But the problem remained John. He was still vehemently opposed to buying the house. You wanted me to persuade him.

"Buying a house in Harare is very risky and unnecessary," John argued when I phoned him.

“Listen, John. You could buy the house for summer vacations in Harare, the sunshine city. Besides, you can rent out the property and earn income in retirement.” There was a brief silence.

“I have misgivings about buying the home. But to save my marriage to Betty, I must support her,” John finally conceded.

I was pleased that John had given in easily, without a protracted argument. In hindsight, I wish I had heeded John’s misgivings.

You went ahead with signing the agreement of sale. You sent me photos of the beautiful house. I congratulated you on the home purchase.

***

Your joy was short lived though. When your cousin ‘died’ and it emerged that you had been conned. It turned out that the photos of the house, the title deeds and agreement of sale were fake. The law firm was dubious and had been struck off the register of law firms for fraud. You had in fact paid for a house that did not exist!

You were devastated and hired another law firm to try and recover your money, but you failed.

I regretted encouraging you to buy the house in Harare.

From then onwards, your life nose-dived. You worked hard to repay the bank loan. But you suffered a mental breakdown and lost your job.

The many arguments with John turned into fist fights and then restraining orders. Your marriage crumbled when the bank auctioned your house to recover the bank loan.

***

Now divorced and alone, you moved into a small, cold council flat. Bouts of depression overwhelmed you, wiping away your once lovely smile.

I often visited you in the small bedsit. You were a heartbreakingly gaunt sight, in stark contrast to your once healthy body.

“You have to eat. Look how much weight you have lost!”

"What is there to live for? I lost my money, my house, and my John."

"You have to pick up the bits and pieces of your life. Who knows, you could find love again."

"Who, in his right mind would want to fall in love with me, an aged, thin and ugly woman with a face full of wrinkles?"

"Don't pity yourself. You just need to eat well, dress properly and go out meeting people."

You stopped the self-pitying.

I bought you plenty of food and beautiful, new clothes. I pleaded with you to put on more flesh. I wanted you to regain your mojo.

"Thank you." You shed tears as we parted. I kept regular phone contact. Sometimes you were happy to talk to me over the phone about the effort you were making to eat, dress up and go out meeting people. I was impressed.

But after some time, you started to ignore my phone calls. You got depressed once more and holed up in your untidy flat. That is when I referred you to Camilla, your social worker. Initially, you resented the intrusion of Camilla. But with time, you grew to like her.

Camilla checked up on you regularly and kept me informed about how you were doing.

I was optimistic that you would rise from the ashes.

***

The day I visited you in St Annes Hospital was the last time I saw you alive. After I left, you swallowed a whole box of Paracetamol tablets. The doctors tried to resuscitate you, but they failed.

You left a brief suicide note.

Dear Kid Simba,

Thanks, but no thanks, for the offer to look after me. Sorry things had to end this way. I am tired of the hard living and want to rest in peace. I hope that one day you will forgive me. Could you please arrange my funeral and cremation? I have a few savings to cover the funeral costs. Scatter my ashes on the Hastings Beach. Keep some of my belongings, donate some to charity shops and dispose the rest in the junk yard.

Bye,

Love Aunt Betty

I was in floods of tears as I held your suicide note in my trembling hands.

***

I am writing this letter, this ode and elegy, to reply to your suicide note and to soothe my aching heart. I want to mourn and celebrate you in equal measure.

It is midnight, on the day you are cremated. Chido, my wife and the two boys, David and Brandon, are in bed. The night is dark and eerie.

I organised your church service as you wished. Only six people attended the service in the small church: the priest, Father Chapman; John; Camilla; two nurses from St Anne's Mental Hospital and me.

The mood during the funeral service was sombre. The peace, the quiet and calm of the service made me feel out of place. I am used to loud African funerals where women wail throughout the night, without civility, and men sit quietly around fires, weeping from the heart.

Father Chapman commenced the service with a prayer committing your weary soul to your creator. In a slow, measured, and authoritative voice, he said, "Betty was a beautiful, funny woman." His blue marble eyes stared back and forth between your coffin and John, sitting in the pew. He said your death was regrettable, but your soul would find joy in the yonder, better world.

I wiped away my tears with my handkerchief at the poignant words of the priest. A lump choked my throat.

When it was my time to deliver a eulogy, I walked tall and straight to the podium. I cleared my groggy throat and sipped water from a glass. I composed myself and gazed at the handful of mourners. I read you a poem titled, "Don't stand at my grave and weep," by an anonymous poet.

I hope you liked the poem and the way I read it. I smothered a tear when I finished reading. In my heart, I was grieving at how you almost gave me a chance to help you, but instead, you chose a different path.

An empty feeling stabbed me in the pith of my stomach as your coffin slid on a conveyor belt into the crematorium and the black curtains were drawn. Cremation is a strange practice to us Africans. Our custom is to bury our dead on a hill. It is a more decent burial than to burn the deceased like chaff. Nevertheless, I respected your dying wish.

After the service, I had a chat with John outside the church.

"Do you remember the day Aunt Betty cat-walked in the lounge, looking like Angela Davis, declaring in a comedic voice, 'Black is Beautiful!'?" John and I burst out laughing.

"If only I had known how much pain our separation caused her, I would have patched up our differences," John said in tears and remorse.

I did not want to accuse John in public or wallow in the helplessness of hindsight. I wanted to "weep before God and laugh before men," as the Jewish proverb says.

I will always miss you, your smile, your sense of humour and your advice as my agony aunt. I forgive you from the deepest chambers of my heart for taking your own life and wish you well. You did what you thought was right. I will forever treasure the day we first met and our close relationship. You brought a cheer to my life at a time of loneliness and uncertainty.

Nothing, not even the pain of death, will take away the treasured, fleeting memories of our precious relationship.

So long, Aunt Betty.

Love,

Kid Simba.

The Man who had the hands of a Baboon

One cloudy, wet morning, I woke up to discover that a thief had broken into my grandmother's chicken run and stolen two chickens.

"*Maiwe! Maiwe!*" My grandmother, VaSekenhamo, cried out. I felt sympathy for her.

"Rwizi, go now and fetch VaGono," she said to me, after wiping tears off her wrinkled cheeks. Besides being the headman, VaGono was also the 'detective' and witchdoctor of Rugare village.

I watched VaGono, his two aides and his dog, Shumba, meticulously examine the crime scene. The hinges of the small wooden door of the chicken run were broken. Inside, white feathers were strewn all over the wet mud. There was a big, cracked footprint in the chicken dung. The other ten chickens in an inner enclosure were untouched.

Shumba, restrained on VaGono's leash, picked the scent of the thief and tracked his movements through the maize fields to Majongwe's homestead. The two aides and I followed behind VaGono and Shumba.

Majongwe was the notorious village thief. The lanky, middle-aged man with an oval-shaped face and small darting chameleon eyes lived with his family in an unattractive homestead with four ramshackled huts. The family was shunned by the entire village.

VaGono knocked hard on the door of the biggest of the four huts. There was momentary silence. Then the hut door creaked and swung open. Out came a dreary-eyed Majongwe.

"Good morning. Do you have anything to do with the theft of two chickens from VaSekenhamo's chicken run?" asked VaGono.

"No. I have nothing to do with that," declared Majongwe, yawning.

"Where were you last night?" interrogated VaGono, glaring into Majongwe's eyes.

I saw Majongwe's eyes shift away from VaGono. "I was at home with my family." Majongwe seemed unsure of himself and trembled slightly.

"Can you explain why my dog, Shumba, has picked your scent from the chicken run and trailed it to your home? Can you also explain why we have tracked your footprint from the chicken run to here?"

"Pure coincidence, I presume," Majongwe muttered.

"We will see about that," said VaGono, unleashing Shumba.

The dog ran through the kitchen hut door and began to sniff animatedly at something wrapped in a newspaper in a white dish.

Majongwe's face turned as pale as a sick man. "I am sorry, I couldn't help it. My family was starving," Majongwe confessed.

"You must pay a fine of three chickens by the end of the month," ordered VaGono. "If you fail to pay the fine, I will hand you over to the ZRP." A deflated and contrite Majongwe nodded his head. We left his homestead.

***

Back at home, I described to VaSekenhamo the look on Majongwe's face when he was caught lying. VaSekenhamo giggled through her yellow teeth. "Majongwe has the hands of a baboon," she said. "His big thieving hands raided my chicken run the same way a hungry baboon raids a maize field."

I learnt from VaSekenhamo that Majongwe, in his boyhood, had begun stealing the wild fruits that other boys had picked and hidden in the soil to hasten their ripeness. He graduated to stealing mice from small hunters' mouse traps. As an adult, he was once caught breaking into an old woman's granary and was fined a goat and publicly humiliated.

The following morning was bright and sunny. I saw Majongwe passing by the footpath close to our homestead. He was armed with a bow and arrows, a spear and an axe and he had four dogs following him. He disappeared into the dense forest.

"I saw Majongwe going hunting," I told VaSekenhamo.

"Since when has Majongwe had the hunting prowess," remarked VaSekenhamo, in stitches.

Majongwe returned the following afternoon from his hunting. It was sweltering that day.

To the surprise of the entire village, Majongwe was trudging on the footpath, heavily laden with the carcass of a big antelope over his shoulder like Jesus carrying the cross. His dogs pranced around and wagged their tails. I gazed until Majongwe had entered the yard of his homestead and was greeted by the claps and ululation of his wife and two teenage children, a boy, and a girl. I admired the hunting prowess of Majongwe that afternoon. But not for long.

VaGono came to our homestead hissing. "A thief has disturbed the animal trap that I had set up in the forest and stolen the animal that had been caught in it. Who from the village went hunting lately?"

"Rwizi, my grandson, saw Majongwe return from hunting with the carcass of an antelope flung over his shoulder," reported VaSekenhamo.

VaGono, his aides and I rushed to Majongwe's homestead.

It is Shona hunting culture that no one should steal an animal caught by someone else's animal trap, lest the thief is cursed by an evil spell cast by the person who set the animal trap. It has been this way for generations.

On arrival at Majongwe's homestead, VaGono knocked hard on the door of the kitchen hut. There was a momentary silence. Then Majongwe, visibly exhausted, emerged from the hut.

"Majongwe, did you steal the animal caught in my trap?" asked VaGono, cutting to the chase.

"No, I didn't steal from your trap. I swear," declared Majongwe.

"Alright, then. Only a real fool steals from the village witchdoctor," said VaGono, leading the way out of Majongwe's homestead.

***

I was there, at VaGono's homestead, when Majongwe publicly confessed to stealing the antelope caught in VaGono's trap. He begged for forgiveness. He even brought his wife and two children.

Majongwe explained that when he and his family ate the meat of the antelope for supper the previous night, their bellies began to swell like they were pregnant. They realised a curse had been put on whoever stole the trapped animal and ate its meat.

VaGono felt deep sympathy for Majongwe and his family. He mixed some of his herbs with water and gave the concoction to Majongwe and his family to drink. The swelling of their bellies stopped. Gradually, their swollen bellies deflated.

Majongwe swore that he would never steal again.

The Madman on First Street

It was a hot Saturday morning in August. I ambled along First Street with Tsitsi, my fiancée. I pecked her on the mouth and fastened my arms around her waist.

First Street was a beehive of activity – newspaper vendors, shop owners, beggars, street preachers and shoppers buzzed along the shopping high street. The smell of fried chips and barbecued meat outside Wimpy restaurant made me salivate like Pavlov's dog. Suddenly, someone bellowed behind us.

I turned around and saw the mad man. As he staggered towards me and Tsitsi, my heart skipped a beat. Adrenaline rushed through my veins and a shudder ran down my spine. I held Tsitsi close to my chest.

The mad man stopped about a metre away from us. He was of medium height. He had the sooty face of a chimney sweeper. He wore a torn and greasy military fatigue and dirty dreadlocks. He smelled like rotten eggs.

"Who is your buyer?" The mad man asked, rolling his marble eyes.

I was quiet. My heart thumped. I avoided direct eye contact with him, shifting my gaze to the shop window display. Tsitsi tightened her grip on my arm. I peeked at her.

"Tell me, who is your buyer?" The mad man raised his voice.

I was mute. I vaguely recalled hearing a voice that sounded like that of the madman sometime, somewhere.

Tsitsi released herself from the grip of my arms and approached the window display outside Barbour's department store. "I would like you to buy me that nine-carat gold ring," she said, ignoring the mad man's presence.

The madman glared at Tsitsi and then at me, from scalp to sole. "Are you husband and wife?"

"None of your business," I blurted out.

The madman scratched his lice-infested head. "You are unmarried and living in sin like prostitutes."

I frowned. "Piss off!" I shooed him away.

The mad man scowled. His face appeared familiar. I recognised the scar under his eye. But I still could not recall where I had met him before.

"You are a dog!" the mad man started yelling, in a sudden frenzy of rage. He cursed my manhood.

I ignored the torrent of insults and turned to Tsitsi. "I think we should go. I do not want to argue with him. There is a full moon these days."

"Ignore him, Chenjerai. Can't you see he is mad?" Tsitsi's eyes were glued to the wedding rings in the window display.

"We must go." I pulled Tsitsi away.

"What's the matter, Chenjerai?"

"I think I have met that madman somewhere." My heart began to beat fast.

"Where? Maybe, it's a case of mistaken identity."

Meanwhile, the madman wandered off, still cursing me.

We walked to a pedestrian bench and I observed him.

He lay prostrate on the dirty pavement, about fifteen metres from where we sat. He mimicked aiming and firing a gun and rolled on the pavement. He stood up and stabbed an invisible person. Then he knelt, asking for forgiveness.

Suddenly, the mad man jumped up and started accosting a woman pushing a buggy with a baby inside. I watched, in horror and disbelief, as the mad man harassed the hapless woman and her baby.

I rushed to the aid of the woman and her baby. "Hey you! Leave them alone!" I pushed away the mad man. He staggered back.

"I will kill you," the mad man shouted, with saliva frothing through his rotten teeth.

"I said leave them alone. Go back to whoever bewitched you!" I was spewing verbal acid.

Onlookers gaped at my confrontation with the madman.

"I will kill you!" The madman raged. He clenched his fists and danced around in a way reminiscent of Muhammad Ali in the boxing ring. "I killed many people in Chiadzwa."

The word, "Chiadzwa" struck me like lightning and I almost fainted. I trembled and breathed heavily. I was in a daze as I staggered back to Tsitsi.

"What is the matter, Chenjerai? You look like you have just seen a ghost," Tsitsi said.

"I know that mad man." I was gasping for air. "He was a Lieutenant Colonel in the army. Lieutenant Colonel Shato. I met him in my village in Chiadzwa. He was the devil incarnate."

"Are you sure, that's him?"

"Yes. I recognised his voice and the scar under his eye. He terrorised, tortured, and shot and killed people in my village in Chiadzwa during the diamond rush. He tortured me once for trading in illegal diamonds."

"Are you really sure that's him?" Tsitsi's eyes bulged.

I nodded.

"What happened to him then?"

"*Ngozi*, the avenging spirits of the people he killed are haunting him, I presume."

***

Lieutenant Colonel Shato commanded a battalion of soldiers sent by the Minister of Defence to take back the alluvial diamond fields of Chiadzwa.

Rampant diamond panners had overrun the fields during the free for all diamond rush. Lieutenant Shato and his battalion had orders to shoot and kill diamond panners refusing to cease the illegal diamond mining.

Within weeks, Lieutenant Shato had become notorious for shooting, detaining, and torturing villagers suspected of panning, aiding and abetting fugitives and shady buyers in the illegal diamond trade. This was the start of 'Operation Hakudzokwi.' Lieutenant Shato warned illegal diamond panners that they would not return home; they would either be shot, injured, admitted to hospital or detained.

My chilling encounter with Lieutenant Shato was when he raided my village one dark night with a handful of soldiers. A hard knock on my village hut door woke me up.

"Who is it?"

"Lieutenant Shato. Open the door."

My heart beat like an African drum as I quickly dressed. I lit a candle with trembling hands, balls of sweat forming on my forehead. I slowly opened the door.

Lieutenant Shato and the soldiers burst through the door. "Are you Chenjerai?" he asked.

"Yes."

"We are reliably informed that you have been selling illegal diamonds. Tell me, who is your buyer?"

"I am not selling illegal diamonds."

"Tell me, who is your buyer?" Lieutenant Shato slapped me hard across the face.

I fell backwards, hitting the floor hard. I saw stars twinkling in my eyes.

"Tell me, who is your buyer?" Lieutenant Shato barked. "We want to know all your buyers."

"I told you, I don't sell illegal diamonds."

"Search this hut!" Lieutenant Shato ordered the soldiers. They searched and found nothing.

"You shall speak." Lieutenant Shato grabbed me by the scruff of my neck and dragged me to the military truck outside. I was driven to Chiadzwa military camp.

There, Lieutenant Shato whipped me with a sjambok. I pleaded with him to let me go because I was not involved in the illegal diamond trade and I was suffering from malaria. But Lieutenant Shato would not stop. "Tell me, who is buying your illegal diamonds?" He whipped me black and blue.

"I don't know anything about illegal trade in diamonds. I'm innocent." I lay on the floor in the torture room, in a pool of urine and blood, writhing in pain.

"You shall speak." Lieutenant Shato's sjambok tore across my back. I bellowed like a wounded bull. Lieutenant Shato kicked me in the head, and I passed out.

I regained consciousness the following morning. My whole body was numb with pain. The malaria fever had got worse. I lapsed in and out of consciousness.

Lieutenant Shato was afraid that I might die at the military base. He ordered my immediate release.

I crawled until I reached the dust road. There, a good Samaritan driving by saw me lying beside the road and he drove me to the hospital.

Eventually, Lieutenant Shato was redeployed away from Chiadzwa military base, after villagers complained to the local member of parliament about his cruelty. Lieutenant Shato had shot and killed a young boy suspected of panning alluvial diamond fields at night. Bullets had ripped the boy's head open. That was the last time Lieutenant Shato was seen or heard of.

***

"This mad man has paid a huge price for his cruel deeds. That is Karma," said Tsitsi. Her countenance was full of sadness. "I think we should go."

"No. Not yet," I said. "I have to confront him about his past cruel deeds."

"No, you can't do that. He is dangerous. He has killed people. He will hurt you," Tsitsi pleaded.

"I will confront him. Wait. I have a plan." I rushed into the OK supermarket on First Street. There, I bought a long rope and tied a noose at one end.

"What is that? What do you want to do with that rope?" Tsitsi was perplexed.

"It's a gift for the madman."

"You must be kidding, right?" Tsitsi could not believe what I had just said.

"Yes, a gift for the madman."

"A gift for what? Chenjerai, don't be silly. Don't confront him," Tsitsi pleaded again.

I mustered courage and approached the mad man. Anger was seething through my veins. The mad man stared at me and then at the sisal rope.

"Do you remember me?" I glared at the madman.

The mad man shook his head.

"I remember you as Lieutenant Shato. You tortured me in Chiadzwa on suspicion of trading in illegal diamonds. You shot and killed many villagers. The diamonds were a source of our livelihood in the village then."

The mad man nodded. He remained quiet.

"Look, now, *ngozi* is tormenting you."

Tears glistened in the madman's eyes. "Please forgive me." He knelt, still begging for forgiveness.

"I am not God, who forgives transgressions." I was shaking with anger.

The madman continued asking for forgiveness. He was contrite.

"You have paid a huge price for your transgressions. This is your comeuppance. So, here is a long rope for you," I said, handing him the rope. "You can hang yourself on a tree the same way Judas did. That should put you out of your misery."

The madman took the rope. He looked at it. He looked at me. His mouth was gaping. I walked away.

I walked back to Tsitsi. I kissed her on the mouth and fastened my arm around her waist. I did not look back at the madman. I was happy that the spirits of the dead had returned to haunt the living for their cruel death.

Crossing the Rubicon

Despite the dangers, Sarudzayi continued secretly meeting the freedom fighters near their military base in Sangodema mountain. The white colonial regime prohibited the villagers from collaborating with "terrorists", their name for the freedom fighters. Any villager defying the order was liable for detention or torture. But Sarudzayi was both defiant and naïve.

She was unperturbed by the order or any of the other risks of collaborating with the freedom fighters. She could be ambushed by the Rhodesian forces at night when sneaking out of the village to meet the freedom fighters, step on landmines or be attacked by wild creatures prowling in the night. Sarudzayi, only seventeen, supported the ongoing war of liberation and dreamt of black majority rule in Rhodesia. She organised a group of twenty girls to collaborate with the freedom fighters. Girls raised less suspicion than boys.

Although Sarudzayi initially dreaded sneaking out at midnight to meet the freedom fighters, she soon mustered the courage. She disappeared into the night with the other village girls. Their heads were laden with big bowls of *sadza* and stew, *nyama,* bread, tea, cigarettes, painkillers and bags of washed and pressed laundry for the freedom fighters.

Sarudzayi led the procession of girls along a footpath that meandered out of Chakanyuka village, down a valley and then up a hill, to the foot of the densely wooded Sangodema Mountain. This was the rendezvous with the freedom fighters. The freedom fighters threatened to punish "sell-outs," villagers they accused of siding with the repressive white colonial regime. For months, Sarudzayi and the other girls evaded the Rhodesian army. Their initial fear of the freedom fighters was gone. Mutual trust had developed between them.

Sarudzayi was fond of listening to the tales of the freedom fighters; how they had left schools, jobs in town and even university to join the war of liberation. Sarudzayi was proud of her own minor role in all of it. However, she did not want to join the war.

Then one day the freedom fighters summoned twenty youths from Chakanyuka village, including Sarudzayi, to a special night meeting, *pungwe*. The meeting would be held at their military base. No one from the village had ever been up the mountain, to the military base. Sarudzayi was worried about the meeting. *Why were adults not invited to the meeting? What did the freedom fighters really want from them?* Sarudzayi did not wish to be labelled a "sell-out" if she did not attend the meeting, so she decided to attend.

"Return home as soon as the meeting is over. I don't want you hanging around with that boy, Durai," VaMarunjata, Sarudzayi's mother, cautioned her. She hugged Sarudzayi and stroked her braided hair.

"Yes, *Amai*. I will do so," Sarudzayi replied. Sometimes she could not stand her mother's overprotectiveness. She wanted a bit more space to breathe. Her mother seemed to always breathe down her neck. Maybe because she was an only child, her mother's precious egg, *zai regondo*. Sarudzayi's mother wanted her to have a good education after the war was over. She did not want her falling pregnant out of wedlock as often happened to most of the village girls.

Sarudzayi waved at her mother who stood fixed to the same spot, observing her and nineteen other boys and girls disappear under the cover of darkness.

"Why do you look so worried?" Durai, a boy from the village, asked Sarudzayi as they walked to the rendezvous with the freedom fighters.

"I have a bad feeling about this meeting. I hope the freedom fighters have not identified a sell-out among us. I hate to see them flog the culprit in front of everyone." Sarudzayi avoided direct eye contact with Durai. She knew he was attracted to her. She was not ready to yield her heart to him.

"Don't worry, Sarudzayi. Maybe the freedom fighters just want to update us on the war effort."

"I hope so."

When Sarudzayi and the other boys and girls arrived at the rendezvous, the freedom fighters were nowhere in sight. Sarudzayi whistled a secret code, to communicate with the freedom fighters. She and the other boys and girls waited patiently in the echoing silence of the dark night.

After ten minutes, thirty freedom fighters, brandishing AK-47s and SKS rifles suddenly emerged from the surrounding thicket bushes like ants coming out of the woodwork. Some of the teenagers froze or cowered.

Comrade Mwanawevhu, the leader of the freedom fighters, thanked the teenagers for coming to the meeting. He quietly led the procession up to the top of Sangodema Mountain, the secret military base. The military base was a cave. The freedom fighters lit a fire inside and commandeered the youths into it. Inside, the cave was big, cold and eerie. Silhouettes danced on the walls. Huge, green wooden crates with weapons and ammunition were strewn on the dusty ground.

Sarudzayi huddled with the other teenagers on empty sack bags laid on the ground. She watched the freedom fighters devour the mountains of *sadza* and *nyama* they had brought them. Today, the freedom fighters were unusually quiet and she was disturbed by their demeanour. She was used to seeing them laughing and joking. There was a tightening sensation in the pith of her stomach.

Are the freedom fighters moving to another base? Have they summoned us to help them carry their weapons? Have the freedom fighters discovered a sell-out among us? Who is the sell-out? Sarudzayi was lost in thought.

After they finished eating, Comrade Mwanawevhu and the other freedom fighters started teaching the teenagers new revolutionary songs and chanting slogans.

Then Comrade Mwanawevhu addressed the teenagers, "I have summoned you to discuss your role in the war of liberation. What are your roles in the on-going war of liberation?"

"To feed you. You have risked your lives to free this country from white colonial rule," Sarudzayi replied.

"Well done, Sarudzayi."

"We are your eyes and ears," Durai chipped in. "We see and hear the activities of the enemy and report to you."

"Thank you, Durai, *Mujibha*. What are the other roles?" There was silence. "We want to recruit teenagers like you to join the war of liberation," declared Comrade Mwanawevhu. "Who wants to join us?"

Sarudzayi was stunned. None of the other teenagers raised a hand. The cave was as silent as a graveyard.

Comrade Mwanawevhu's big, bulging eyes glared at the teenagers. "We have observed your conduct, over the months, and we decided to recruit you for guerrilla training. Your country needs you at this hour. Does anyone have a question?"

There were mutterings of shocked disbelief.

Comrade Mwanawevhu scowled at the teenagers. "Does anyone have a question?" He raised his voice, pointing his glinting rifle at them.

Sarudzayi was trembling and sweating. The other boys and girls began to whimper like puppies. Sarudzayi was petrified, but she mustered the courage to raise her hand. "You know that joining the war is a difficult decision to make. Let us return home and inform our parents and seek their blessings."

"We will not allow you to return home," declared Comrade Mwanawevhu. "You have seen the location of this military base. You will sell out the location of this base. Then the Rhodesian helicopters will bomb us." His voice was raised, with a timbre of anger.

"Please grant me one last chance to bid farewell to my mother," Sarudzayi pleaded, sobbing.

"I said, you are not returning to your parents," Comrade Mwanawevhu reiterated. There was a frenzy of sobs by the teenagers.

"We will be leaving this military base tonight."

"Where are you taking us?" Sarudzayi quizzed, with floods of tears.

"We will be travelling through the night to the next rendezvous, the bus stop. We should reach it before dawn. There, we will board a bus to Mozambique," Comrade Mwanawevhu replied.

The word 'Mozambique' hit Sarudzayi like a meteor out of the blue. She was inconsolable, gutted by what felt like the ultimate act of betrayal.

We welcomed the freedom fighters and provided them with food. And this is how they repay our hospitality? Abduction at gunpoint! What will happen to my mother when she finds out that I have been abducted? What will happen to my mother and the other villagers when the Rhodesian army learn that we have joined the 'terrorists?' Will I ever see my mother alive again? These questions gnawed on Sarudzayi's mind.

Sarudzayi blubbered at the thought of leaving the life of Chakanyuka village. She had fond memories of playing childhood games like *nhodo* with other girls, fetching water and firewood, gossiping about boys, the growing pains of adolescence and the love of her mother. She missed school days and playing games in the school grounds. The schools had long been shut due to the war. Now she was leaving the only life she had ever known and loved. She was being forced to join the war at gunpoint.

The petrified teenagers were ordered to carry cooking pans, water cans, military equipment and ammunition and other loads.

Before setting off, Comrade Mwanawevhu warned the teenagers, "If you try to escape, I will shoot you without blinking and bury you in a shallow grave for the wild animals. Do not test me. You will regret it." Comrade Mwanawevhu aimed his AK-47 at the terrified teenagers. His eyes were bloodshot.

Sarudzayi was mute with fear. She loathed Comrade Mwanawevhu like she hated Lucifer.

The procession set off through the tall grass and bushy undergrowth. The darkness camouflaged them from the patrolling Rhodesian forces. One armed freedom fighter led the way, with another at the rear. The other twenty-eight-armed freedom fighters flanked the teenagers on either side.

Sarudzayi was terrified of being ambushed by the Rhodesian forces. The howls of hyenas tore through the night and sent a shiver down her spine. "May I please have a drink of water?" Sarudzayi asked one freedom fighter next to her in the procession. They had been walking for an hour.

"No. We have to conserve the small quantity of water we have. You will get some when we reach the next stop," replied the freedom fighter.

Sarudzayi was upset but she quietly trudged on, thirsty and heavy laden.

"Come on, move it!" A freedom fighter barked at a tired boy who had stopped walking. He hit the boy with the butt of his AK47. The boy groaned in agony.

Sarudzayi pitied him. She began to plot an escape at an opportune time.

***

It was dawn when they arrived at the next stop. It was another cave in the middle of the dense forest. One of the freedom fighters entered the cave first with his torch to inspect it, then lit a fire.

The boys and girls were ordered into the smaller, dark cave. The cave smelled musty and earthy. The air was humid and the walls were damp. There was more ammunition stored in the cave. There were tin cans and burnt cigarette butts on the dusty ground. It appeared the freedom fighters had used the cave before.

Sarudzayi was sweaty. She was relieved to put down her heavy load. Her legs were painful, tired and swollen. She was offered a sip of water by one of the freedom fighters. After everyone had consumed the small food rations, Comrade Mwanawevhu addressed the exhausted teenagers. "This is the bus stop. Tomorrow we will board the bus to Mozambique."

Sarudzayi was perplexed. There was no bus stop in the middle of the dense forest! Immediately, she realised that the freedom fighters had lied to them. She knew that the journey to Mozambique would be on foot. Sarudzayi grew more determined to escape.

The following morning, Sarudzayi fidgeted under a tree, outside the cave. She was looking for the opportune moment to bolt. Suddenly, there was the drone of a helicopter approaching the cave from the west. The freedom fighters ordered everyone into the cave.

Soon, the helicopter was hovering above the cave. Its deafening drone petrified Sarudzai. She was numb with fear and held her breath.

"Do not move!" Comrade Mwanawevhu ordered everyone. The Rhodesian Air Force 1978 Bell Helicopter 206B hovered above them, circling the base twice before it flew away. Sarudzayi sighed as its drone faded in the distance. The freedom fighters ordered the teenagers to remain inside the cave.

Sarudzayi was gutted. She had missed an opportunity to escape. Now it would be harder to escape with freedom fighters constantly guarding the exit of the cave. She would devise another escape plan.

At nightfall, the freedom fighters went out on a reconnaissance. The Rhodesian forces had moved out of the area. The freedom fighters ordered the teenagers to pack luggage, equipment, ammunition and weapons. The procession moved to the next military base.

***

The third military base, Chombo base, was a staging point where heavier equipment and artillery was stored. Thousands of recruits were trained and vetted there for advanced military training. Trained cadres returning from Mozambique were also based there and received their final orders of deployment to areas of combat.

Sarudzayi persuaded Durai to meet her in secret. They met behind a huge baobab tree. It was prohibited for the teenagers to meet and form relationships.

"Durai, will you please escape with me?" Sarudzayi pleaded.

"Saru, are you out of your mind? Escape? Where to?" Durai was astounded.

"Home."

"There is no longer a home for us to return to. Our village has probably been razed to the ground by Rhodesian forces. Besides, if we return home, the Rhodesian forces will arrest us for collaborating with the freedom fighters."

"We could escape to Salisbury."

"How will we get there?"

"We will walk."

"Walk two hundred kilometres? You know there are plenty of roadblocks during the day and curfews at night."

"I know."

"Do you have any money?"

"No."

"What would happen if the freedom fighters caught us trying to escape?"

"I don't know."

"They will torture and kill us. Set an example of us. Have you considered what would happen if Rhodesian forces captured us?"

"No."

"They will interrogate us and extract intelligence on the location of the bases of the freedom fighters. We will become traitors to the cause of our people. After the interrogation, they will kill us and dump our bodies in the jungle."

"I see."

"Why are you trying to escape in the first place? Weren't you the one who loved to collaborate with the freedom fighters? What did you think would be the end result?"

"I loved to offer them assistance. But I did not want to join the army."

"So, what shall we do?" Sarudzayi was frustrated by Durai; he was playing devil's advocate.

"We need to stay put in the meantime."

Sarudzayi was disappointed. She realised that it was now impossible to return to Chakanyuka village. Her mother was probably languishing in a Rhodesian prison because her daughter had joined the 'terrorists'. She would also be charged with the crime of not reporting the presence of the 'terrorists' in the vicinity of the village. She begged Durai to meet her again to discuss the matter of escaping and conjure up an escape plan. They parted ways.

***

The longer Sarudzayi remained at Chombo military base, the more she began to change her mind about escaping. She was indoctrinated with war propaganda. She realised that she had no other viable option left than to join the war of liberation. Gradually, she became more committed to liberating Rhodesia.

During the orientation classes, Sarudzayi developed public speaking skills of addressing masses of people, the *povho*, and raising their morale. She began to love doing the military drills, handling and assembling rifles. She developed a better knowledge and understanding of the colonial history of Rhodesia and the ideals of the war of liberation.

Comrade Mwanawevhu grew to respect Sarudzayi for her commitment, discipline and leadership in military training.

The memories of her mother and growing up in Chakanyuka village began to fade away from Sarudzayi's mind. She assumed the *Chimurenga* name, *Comrade Sarudzayi Zvenyika*. She was among the top sixteen recruits, selected by Comrade Mwanawevhu, for advanced guerrilla training in Mozambique.

Sarudzayi was pleased by the recognition of her hard work in training. But sadly, Durai, her friend and secret admirer, stayed behind at Chombo base. He would follow with the next cohort of recruits. Their secret meetings had developed into a love relationship. Love blossoming in the bush like a Flame Lilly. She vowed to rekindle their romance when he joined her in Mozambique.

***

At dawn, four freedom fighters, Sarudzayi and her cohort of fifteen military trainees set off for the Zambezi River. It was a four-hour walk. The group arrived at the river in the early morning. The freedom fighters surveyed the Zambezi valley with their binoculars. There was no sign of Rhodesian forces. The valley was deserted.

The freedom fighters uncovered four canoes hidden in thicket bushes close to the riverbank. They divided the recruits into four groups, one freedom fighter leading each group. Each group waded into the raging Zambezi River.

Initially, Sarudzayi was afraid of crossing the mighty Zambezi River which teemed with hungry crocodiles. But she gathered courage and pushed the canoe into the river till the water was knee high. She heaved herself into the canoe with her team. Sarudzayi stole a last glance at the Rhodesian side of the Zambezi River. It dawned on her that she had reached a point of no return. She was crossing the Rubicon. She was going to train to fight and liberate her country from colonial rule.

As the canoe drifted downstream, towards the Indian Ocean, Sarudzayi's team rowed and glided, avoiding the rapids. Sarudzayi felt dislocated from everything she ever knew and loved; Chakanyuka village, her mother, friends and Durai. She faced an uncertain future ahead of her. But there was no turning back. She would continue to soldier on until Rhodesia was free from white minority colonial rule. She had sacrificed her life for the struggle for independence of the black majority in Rhodesia. Tears sparkled in her eyes. Although a lump choked her throat, Sarudzayi's determination to liberate her country emboldened her.

The Miniskirt March

Pamela was adamant that the march planned for Saturday morning should go ahead. She had heard loud voices opposing the march, but she had publicly defended her right to lead the march, in the media. Nevertheless, Pamela feared, inwardly, that the march could turn ugly, and demonstrators could get hurt.

The march was to challenge the misogyny of commuter omnibus drivers and touts that harassed women wearing miniskirts in the Harare city centre. Public opinion was divided. Some young women supported the march because it raised awareness and challenged the harassment of women wearing miniskirts.

Detractors opposed the planned demonstration. "The demonstration is not necessary. These young women should just cover up, rather than walk the streets, half-dressed in miniskirts. They are inviting the harassment," they said. Others argued, "there are more pressing issues to demonstrate about in the city than miniskirts. Why not demonstrate about uncollected refuse, contaminated tap-water and corruption in the city council instead?" Others coined a pejorative term for the planned demonstration: "The Miniskirt March."

The more the opposition against the march grew, the more Pamela grew determined to lead the demonstration. She was the leader of a women's rights group in Harare.

***

The day of the march was wet, cold and cloudy. The musty smell of Jacaranda tree leaves diffused in the air. The city was bustling with shoppers, traders, demonstrators and street kids.

Hundreds of women from all walks of life congregated outside the Harare Mayor's town house, in the city centre. The rainbow of women ranged from Africans, Coloureds and Whites, young and middle-aged. All the women donned miniskirts of assorted colours on their varying body shapes and sizes; slim, trim, curvy, stout, flabby, tall and short. There were different styles of miniskirts: mods, flirty, kinky, sporty, and formal. Some demonstrators matched the miniskirts with tights and high heels.

The morning was abuzz with thumping drum beats, deafening whistles and songs of solidarity with female victims of gender-based harassment.

The demonstrators held up placards with different messages:

"Real men don't harass women"

"It's my right to wear a miniskirt"

"My body, not your body"

"Your lust is not my problem"

"Women reclaiming Harare streets."

Passers-by looked on, bewildered by the pomp and frenzy of the marchers.

***

Pamela, young, tall, with dark, smooth-textured skin stood on the steps of the Mayor's town house. She had long braids tied into a ponytail. She wore a leopard-striped top and a black miniskirt, contrasted by white tights and black Dr. Martens boots. Her miniskirt rode high above the knees. She had a black belt in Karate.

Pamela cleared her throat and surveyed the demonstrators. "Quiet, please! Quiet, please!" She spoke through the loudspeaker. A pin dropping could be heard in the ensuing silence.

"Thank you, sisters, women, *madzimai*, for coming to support this march," Pamela began, "We are sick and tired of all these cases of women being harassed by commuter omnibus drivers and touts in this city for wearing miniskirts. Enough is enough! We are here to send a clear message, 'Stop harassing women!' Women must feel free to walk the streets of Harare wearing whatever they want. Today we will march into the lion's den and poke the lion in the face." Wild cheers erupted. Drums thumped and whistles blew.

Pamela, emboldened by the demonstrators, proceeded, "We will march along Julius Nyerere Way, then turn at Speke Avenue, at State Lottery Hall. Then we will march on to Copacabana bus terminal. There, we will confront the minibus drivers and touts. We will then proceed along Chinhoyi Street to Market Square terminal. Do not be afraid. The police are here to escort us."

There was a roar of approval and clapping of hands.

"Women of this city must unite and ignite! Let us start marching." Pamela concluded, firing up the demonstrators.

The demonstrators started marching behind the police escort; two police officers on motorbikes, and five police officers on foot with two dogs. The singing and chanting reverberated along Julius Nyerere way, drowning the sounds of the Saturday morning traffic whizzing through the city.

Passers-by reacted differently to the demonstrators. Some glared, in shocked disbelief, shook their heads and quietly walked away. Some smiled, cheered on the demonstrators and fist-pumped in solidarity with the demonstrators. Others yelled insults and jeered at the demonstrators.

***

The singing grew louder as the demonstrators approached Copacabana. The snail pace of the demonstrators at the busy commuting hour resulted in a traffic jam. Drivers sounded car horns impatiently. Pamela led the singing and dancing, in front of the demonstrators.

"Hey, you prostitute! Get out of the way!" An irate minibus driver shouted at Pamela.

Pamela jeered at him. The other demonstrators also jeered at him.

"Who are you calling a prostitute?" Pamela asked the driver. "Maybe your mother is the prostitute," Pamela shot back. She waved her placard, written, **"Real men don't harass women"** at the windscreen of the minibus.

Other demonstrators joined Pamela, *toyi-toyi* dancing around the minibus. The atmosphere was degenerating into a frenzy of anger. The police escorts stepped in before the confrontation got out of hand. They ordered the demonstrators to make way for the minibus. The demonstrators marched on, singing, jeering and yelling insults at passing commuter omnibuses. Pamela yelled, "You are not real men. Real men don't harass women!"

A commuter minibus driver yelled, "Gumbura should be freed from prison, so that he teaches you prostitutes a lesson." He was referencing a notorious church pastor jailed for sexually abusing his female congregants.

Pamela broke into a song, "*Wakatadza kutengera mai vako miniskirt, haunyare*!" She berated the men for failing to buy their own mothers miniskirts. The demonstrators joined in the singing. Some bemused men made obscene gestures at the demonstrators.

"Our African women are being misled by European culture," complained one man, shaking his head. The demonstrators soldiered on, singing and dancing.

"You are all prostitutes! Married women don't behave like you lot," another man yelled.

The demonstrators jeered at him and continued marching and singing.

"We are tired of AIDS and these *slay queens*," another man protested.

Pamela broke into another song, "Omnibus drivers and touts change your hearts!"

Suddenly, two men emerged from an alley and charged toward Pamela. One of the men threw a punch at her. Pamela dodged the punch and hit him in the back of the head with the loudspeaker she was holding. The other man tried to yank Pamela's braids, but she ducked and threw a Roundhouse kick into his head.

"Bloody scum!" Pamela was karate posing in stances like Angela Mao.

"You think you are smart, prancing around in your miniskirt," barked one man. He tried to grab Pamela's miniskirt. Pamela slapped him in the face and pushed him away. Immediately, the other demonstrators descended on the two men like a swarm of bees.

"Perverts! How dare you do this!" An angry demonstrator screamed, beating the two men with a stick. The men cowered then fled from the demonstrators. A police officer ran after the two men.

Pamela regained her composure. Her heart was beating like a Conga. Quickly, she mustered up courage and continued singing and chanting. She did not want to exude weakness in front of the other demonstrators.

The demonstrators marched on towards Market Square. A drunk man yelled at them, "*Mudzoke kana mapurisa aenda muzoona zvinoitika.*" He dared the women to return when the police officers had gone.

"Why are you marching in those miniskirts like prostitutes?" Another man quizzed.

"Bloody idiot! Bloody shit!" Pamela shot back, making obscene gestures at him.

The man shouted back, "Are you on special offer? Buy one, get one free?"

"You are a rabid dog!" yelled Pamela.

"The President and the ruling party shouldn't be allowing you to parade yourselves like prostitutes," the man remarked.

Pamela began to shimmy in front of him. The dumbfounded man froze, his face contorted with contempt. Pamela ran back to the front of the demonstration. The demonstrators continued singing, chanting slogans and dancing.

At Market Square, a small group of rowdy street kids yelled insults at the demonstrators, "Prostitutes! Prostitutes!"

"Your mothers are the prostitutes!" Pamela shot back, charging towards the street kids. One of the street kids picked up a stone and threw it at Pamela. The stone missed Pamela by an inch. Pamela froze. Her heart missed a beat. One of the police escorts unleashed his dog on the street kids.

The street kids bolted down an alleyway like startled mice, the police dog in hot pursuit. The dog eventually let them go and returned. The demonstrators yelled in triumph. The commuter omnibus station was deserted.

Pamela stood on a platform and silenced the demonstrators. "You saw how those two perverts tried to strip me in public? Enough is Enough! Today, we have shown the men that we will not be bullied. We will not cower in silence. Women in this city have a right to wear miniskirts and feel safe."

There was a rapturous applause. Pamela left the platform. Other women took turns addressing the demonstrators. Every speaker urged the mayor and the police to protect women from harassment on the streets of Harare.

Meanwhile, a reporter waded through the demonstrators to Pamela. "I'm from The Herald newspaper. Could you answer a few questions?"

"Sure," Pamela smiled. "The press is more than welcome to cover our march."

"What exactly do you think you have achieved with this march?"

"We have stood up and spoken out," Pamela declared. "Women of this city have rights. This includes wearing miniskirts without fear of harassment."

"Do you think the harassment will stop, after the demonstration?"

"I hope so," Pamela replied. "The Chinese proverb says, 'the journey of a thousand miles starts with a single step.' This is a first step."

"Young woman, you have not achieved anything," an elderly man suddenly interrupted the conversation. "You have made fools of yourself."

Pamela turned to the elderly man, looking at him from scalp to sole. "We have made our voices heard."

"You shouldn't imitate European styles of dressing," the elderly man warned.

Pamela ignored him and turned back to the reporter. "This is the patriarchy we live with, day in, day out." The reporter nodded.

"Real women must not wear miniskirts," the elderly man declared.

Pamela turned back to the elderly man. "Didn't men and women wear *nhembe* in the 1890s?"

"Yes, they did. But we are not in the 1890s, when people wore short, animal skin kilts. We are in 2019," replied the elderly man.

"Did men back then harass their women as some men do today? I don't think so." Pamela's eyes were bulging.

"What I am saying is, dress up properly, not in these miniskirts," the elderly man pointed at Pamela's miniskirt. "We should see the difference between you, young woman, and the prostitutes in the avenues."

"I have a right to wear what I want, when I want." Pamela declared, cat walking.

"But freedom comes with responsibility, young woman. I can't just walk around the streets exposing my manhood, because I live in a free country," the elderly man retorted.

"How would you feel, if your daughter was harassed for wearing a miniskirt in the city centre?" Pamela quizzed him.

"No. My daughter won't even dare leave my house dressed like that. I will not allow it. She is not a prostitute," the elderly man said.

"Who told you that women who wear miniskirts are prostitutes?" Pamela was irate.

"So, what are they? What has got into you, women, since that Beijing Women's Conference?" He shook his head.

"The world has changed for the better. Women's rights are upheld and protected around the world," Pamela declared. Pamela's mobile phone suddenly rang. She excused herself from the conversation.

Moments later Pamela returned to the platform, beaming. "I had a call from the police. They have arrested the two men who attacked me earlier on. They want me to provide a witness statement at the charge office."

Wild screams and ululation erupted. The demonstrators danced and pranced around in jubilation. They praised the police officers. The elderly man quietly walked away. Pamela thanked all the demonstrators for coming to lend their support for the demonstration.

As Pamela drove to the charge office, she felt mixed emotions. She was overjoyed because the demonstration had achieved its objective; of raising awareness for the plight of young women who were being harassed daily by commuter omnibus drivers and touts for wearing miniskirts. Pamela was relieved that none of the demonstrators was hurt during the skirmishes.

"Bloody men!" Pamela muttered to herself, as she recounted the ogling of commuter omnibus drivers, touts and passers-by, during the demonstration. She choked with anger when she recalled the attack by the two men. Her blood boiled. But now there was poetic justice; she had the last laugh as the two men would be charged for the physical assault in public.

The demonstration was just a step in a journey of a thousand miles to gender equality, Pamela thought. Many more battle lines would be drawn. Many more battles would be fought against the patriarchal structures. Many more victories and frustrations lay ahead. Today was a day of victory. Pamela smiled to the bittersweet victory.

A Mum Indeed

Rumbidzayi's nightmare began with the voicemail message left on her iPhone. Her mind was numbed by fear as she replayed the short message, "Good morning, Ms Gondo. This is Mr Jones, Headteacher of Homeward Grammar School. There has been an incident involving your son, David. Could you please come immediately and collect him from the school?"

Rumbidzayi's blood pressure shot up. She left work and sped off to the boarding school, forty miles away. Many questions troubled her mind as she cruised along the motorway: *What had happened at the school? Was David being racially abused? Was it serious? Yes, it must be serious. Otherwise, Mr Jones would not have asked her to collect David from the school immediately. Was David hurt?*

As she entered the school's towering gates, Rumbidzayi felt intimidated by the beautiful Gothic, Victorian and Regency buildings dotted around the property, the lush lawns, manicured hedges and expensive cars in the car park. She briefly waited in the reception area with wood panelled walls adorned with large, framed classical paintings of DaVinci and Rembrandt.

Then she was directed to Mr Jones' office by a plump, white receptionist with a Vila Petite maxi dress with frilled sleeves, in polka dot. She knocked softly on the door. Her heart started palpitating when she entered the large, well-ventilated office with large, framed pictures of previous head teachers on the walls. Balls of sweat formed on her forehead.

"Thank you for coming at such short notice, Ms. Gondo," said Mr Jones, a slender, stern-looking white man with a pointed nose and glasses that had bi-focal lenses. He gave her a bland smile and gestured to an empty chair.

Mr Jones adjusted his bow tie and cleared his throat. "I am afraid there has been a safeguarding incident in the school, involving the circulation of an image of a schoolgirl. I am sorry to inform you that your son is one of three boys implicated in the safeguarding incident."

"Image? What sort of image?"

"A nude image."

"What? You are saying my son, David, has been involved in circulating a nude image of a schoolgirl?" Rumbidzayi rolled her eyes.

"Yes. Not only that, David and his two friends were also trolling the schoolgirl on social media."

"How can that be? I know my son, he would never do such disgusting things. This must be a big mistake." Rumbidzayi shook her head.

"I'm afraid not. I have evidence that David and his two school friends were indeed involved in the incident."

"What evidence?"

"The image on the mobile phone and messages exchanged on social media accounts."

"The other boys, are they white?"

"Yes."

"Have you considered that maybe my black son is being falsely accused by the two white boys?"

"No, that is not the case, Ms. Gondo. My school does not tolerate racism. In fact, David admitted to receiving the nude image from one of the boys and sharing it with the other boy."

Rumbidzayi went quiet as a Nun.

Mr Jones leaned forward and looked Rumbidzayi directly in the eyes. "My duty is to protect the reputation of the school and safeguard the welfare of all our students. As a result, I have decided to suspend your son and the other two boys, pending a full investigation."

"How can you do that, suspending David, less than six months before GCSE exams?"

"This is a serious matter."

"Oh my God, suspension!" Rumbidzayi put her right hand over her mouth. "How long is the suspension?"

"Two weeks. After that, the school management board will decide, based on the findings and recommendations of our investigation, whether to keep David and the other two boys in school or permanently exclude them. Do you have any further questions?"

"Have you reported the incident to the police?"

"No. We have referred it to children's services instead. We will conduct our own independent investigation. We want to maintain confidentiality and protect the reputation of the school. We do not want the tabloid press swarming us. I urge you not to talk to journalists while the investigation is ongoing."

"Of course not." Tears trickled down Rumbidzayi's cheeks covered in foundation. "My God, suspension!" She stood up and walked out of the office, dazed. David was waiting outside the door. He looked down when Rumbidzayi glared at him.

Rumbidzayi wobbled ahead of David back to the car. She stopped outside and eyed him as if he were a feral child. She finally opened the door and slumped into the driver's seat, sighing.

During the drive home, Rumbidzayi did not talk to David, who sat quietly in the back seat. She was too exhausted and emotionally drained to interrogate him. She bottled the rage that was fizzing inside her, holding the steering wheel tightly as she cogitated. Occasionally, she stole a glance at David through the rear-view mirror.

He avoided eye contact. His eyes were red and swollen.

At home, Rumbidzayi sat alone at the dinner table, quietly eating a ham sandwich. David locked himself in his bedroom.

She went to bed early that night. She lay awake, on top of the duvet wishing the nightmare would be over by the following morning.

***

At 7:30am, Rumbidzayi knocked on David's bedroom door. "We need to talk." David followed her to the kitchen. He yawned and rubbed his eyes.

"Tell me the truth, what really happened at school?"

"A girl from school called Isabel sent a nude picture of herself to my friend, Moses, because she fancied him. Moses was shocked, but thought it was really funny."

"What is funny about that?"

"The way Isabel was proposing to him."

"How did you get yourself involved in all this?"

"Moses sent me the image."

"Why? Why didn't you delete it or send it back?"

"I don't know."

"Then what happened?"

"John, my other friend, coerced me to send him the image. Mum, I did not know what he would do with the image. He photoshopped it and started trolling Isabel on Facebook and Instagram, calling her a whore."

"Why did you share the image with John?"

"He coerced me to share the image. I didn't know he would be so malicious."

"Why, David, why did you do it?"

"I really don't know, mum."

"How did Mr Jones find out about the incident?"

"Isabel reported the incident to the Safeguarding Lead after the gossip spread around the school. The Safeguarding Lead then reported it to Mr Jones. Mr Jones interrogated us, seized our mobile phones and demanded to see our Facebook and Instagram accounts. He accused us of bringing the name of the school into disrepute and decided to suspend us."

"Why, David? Why did you get yourself involved in the first place?"

"I thought it was just banter with the boys at the time. No harm was intended."

"Look how far the banter has taken you. Look how much harm you have done to the poor girl, the school's reputation, yours and my reputation."

"Sorry, mum."

"Sorry won't change anything now. God forbid, the school reports the matter to the police or permanently excludes you and your friends."

"I want to go back to school, mum."

Rumbidzayi shook her head and looked at David. "I came all the way from Zimbabwe to live and work in England and give you the good life I never had. I have been working hard to send you to a good boarding school. And this is how you repay me?"

"Sorry, mum."

"Do you want to end up a fool like your dad who walked out on us for another woman?"

"No, mum."

"Didn't I teach you to respect girls and women?"

"Yes, mum."

"Times have changed, David. In this Me-Too movement era, men are accountable for misogyny and sexual harassment. Look at Harvey Weinstein."

"I am really sorry, mum."

"I want you to write a letter of apology to Isabel."

"Yes, mum." Rumbidzayi grabbed her car keys and stormed out of the house.

***

Mr Jones summoned Rumbidzayi back to the school after two weeks. He looked daggers at Rumbidzayi, inside his office. He shuffled the papers piled up in front of him and cleared his throat. "Our investigation has found out that your son and the other two students breached the school's rules and regulations regarding acceptable behaviour and safeguarding. The boys cyber bullied the schoolgirl. I am sorry to inform you that the school's management board has decided to permanently exclude David and the other boys from the school. We must be strict and set a good example on such serious incidents. My duty is to protect the reputation of the school and safeguard the welfare of all our students."

"No," Rumbidzayi protested. "David has never broken any school rules before this incident. Besides, he says he was coerced into sharing the image. David is also a victim of peer influence. He admitted to his misdemeanour and wrote a letter of apology to the schoolgirl involved. He deserves a second chance."

"I'm sorry, Ms. Gondo, David committed a serious breach of the school's policies. We have a zero-tolerance policy on cyber bullying. Hence, the decision to permanently exclude the boys from this school."

"Permanently exclude? In other words, you are expelling them. What about the girl? Are you also going to permanently exclude her from school? Didn't she start these shenanigans in the first place?"

"The school is yet to make a decision on her."

"I am sorry that the poor girl felt humiliated and violated when the image started circulating. But the fact remains, she started it. She should also be accountable for her actions. I do not condone voyeurism and cyber bullying against girls and women, but David was a victim of peer influence. It must be quite confusing for these children to be developing into adolescents in an over-sexualised culture. We need to empathise and counsel them. David deserves a second chance to redeem himself. He shouldn't be expelled."

"I am sorry. Sometimes, we have to make right decisions and in this case it is protecting the reputation of the school and safeguarding the welfare of other students."

"Please, give my David a second chance. He has less than six months to sit for his GCSEs," Rumbidzayi pleaded.

"I am sorry, Ms. Gondo, the school has already made a decision. Your son should vacate the school premises within an hour. It's your parental responsibility to find him another school."

Rumbidzayi's eyes filled with tears as she stood up and left the office. *It's so unfair. Why did the school decide to expel my David on his first misdemeanour? Didn't he deserve a second chance, with six months before sitting for his GCSEs? Why didn't the school provide her advice on what to do after David's permanent exclusion?* Questions stabbed her mind like spears. Rumbidzayi wiped away the tears with the back of her hand.

***

After crying for days, Rumbidzayi pulled herself together and resolved to never give up on her son, even if everybody else did. She visited another school, a comprehensive school, seeking a place for David to sit for his GCSEs. But the headteacher declined to admit David. He did not want "to take risks with a student permanently excluded for voyeurism and cyberbullying."

Rumbidzayi stormed out of the headteacher's office. "How dare he call my David a voyeur and cyber bully! Yes, my son committed a misdemeanour, but he is neither a voyeur nor a cyber bully. He was a victim of peer influence. I will not give up on him," she muttered to herself and sighed.

At the next comprehensive school, Rumbidzayi wept in front of the headteacher as she narrated David's permanent exclusion from the boarding school. The headteacher took pity on her and agreed to admit David, on condition that he underwent counselling on safeguarding and risks of cyberbullying.

Rumbidzayi waved her hands in the air with joy, delighted that David had been given a second chance to redeem himself. But her joy was short-lived. She observed that David struggled to settle into the new school. She surmised that he still missed the boarding school and his old friends and he still felt a lingering sense of shame and guilt hanging over him. Pain stabbed her heart at seeing David struggling to settle in his new school.

So, Rumbidzayi supported David during the process of adjusting to the new school. She provided him with financial rewards and positive feedback as he progressed with his learning. She was delighted when David made new friends in the new school. Eventually, David went on to pass eight GSCEs. Rumbidzayi ululated when David showed her his GCSE results. She felt vindicated.

***

One day, Rumbidzai was baking a cake when David walked into the kitchen. "Where are you going, all dressed up?"

"I have a date, mum. Her name is Rachel."

"I see." A lump suddenly formed in Rumbidzayi's throat. Her countenance fell.

"What is the matter, mum?"

"Nothing." Tears glistened in Rumbidzayi's eyes.

"What is the matter, mum?"

"Sorry, I remembered your expulsion from the boarding school. I could not help but tear up. You have come an awfully long way, my son, to regain your self-confidence." Rumbidzayi wiped away the tears with the back of her hand. She felt embarrassed, crying in front of David. She hugged him.

"I couldn't have made it without you, the best mum in the world. A mum in need is a mum indeed. Don't worry mum, I will respect Rachel."

"I love you. I am proud of you." Rumbidzayi smiled.

"Thanks, mum."

"Enjoy your date." Rumbidzayi blew a kiss towards David. She felt the lump suddenly disappear from her throat.

Baptism of Fire

The Sunday morning I left home for boarding school, I stole one of my mother's long, sharp silver kitchen knives. I concealed the knife at the bottom of my big, black school trunk. Knives were not allowed at Christian Hope boarding school, but I carried the knife anyway. When I got off the school bus, it was late on a sweltering afternoon.

The boarding master, Mr Dondo, a grumpy, stubby old man with grey hair, welcomed us all Form One students to our new secondary school.

Christian Hope boarding school was in a remote, dusty countryside, hidden behind thick, lush green bushes and elephant grass. The school buildings were old, their cream paint peeling off. It was a far cry from the well-maintained city schools, but Christian Hope had a reputation for producing good academic results. That is why parents chose it.

The dormitories were as small as prison cells with two undersize beds on opposite ends of each room. Cheap smelly blankets covered the beds. The rooms felt like furnaces due to the aluminium roofing.

When my roommate, Kuda, left the room, I took the knife from the trunk and hid it under a mattress. I lay on the small bed, thinking about my cosy bed at home, my FIFA 2022 video game and Play Station. I wasn't in the mood to make new friends.

In the evening, I sat sullen at a long, white table in the brightly lit school dining hall. All the new students were quietly huddled around the table.

Senior students sat on another long table opposite us. They were gesturing at us, giggling and muttering, "I want my mummy."

I felt humiliated. I couldn't eat the hard *sadza* served with greens and beans.

One tall, stocky, ugly senior student kept shouting, "The Freshman has peace in the day, but trouble comes in the night."

I dashed back to my dormitory.

***

Feeling more secure, I opened the lunchbox packed with a mouth-watering, home cooked meal; rice and roasted chicken that my mother had prepared. Suddenly, the ugly senior student from the dining room and four other senior students burst into my room.

"Kid, I am Warlord," announced the senior student, "and these are my gang members."

"I am Simbarashe," I said. Warlord snatched my lunch box and began eating the food.

"Give me back my food. Why are you doing this?" I tried to put on a brave face.

"Because I can," Warlord said, biting into a chicken drumstick. He shared the food with his gang. I shivered helplessly.

"And who have we got here?" Warlord asked, standing over my roommate, Kuda.

Kuda pretended not to hear him. His head was under the blankets. Warlord poured my jug of water over him.

"What are you doing?" Kuda jumped out of bed. Warlord and his gang were in stitches.

I remembered my mum's kitchen knife. I considered reaching for it but thought better of it.

"I will report you to the boarding master," I declared.

"Cheeky kid," said Warlord. "Your life at this school will be hell if you do that." Warlord was breathing into my face. After eating all my food, Warlord and his gang left.

"I will report this incident to the boarding master," I told Kuda.

"Don't. No, Simbarashe, don't," pleaded Kuda. "Bullying always happens when you are a freshman in boarding school. Things will get better."

I reported the incident to Mr Dondo, the boarding master, anyway, and he promised to investigate.

On the following day, Monday morning, the first day of the school term, Warlord and his gang ordered that I be the last one to get into the showers. Eventually, when my turn came, there was no more hot water. The cold water cut through my spine.

Warlord confronted me at breakfast in the dining room. "Kid, you are a dead boy walking. I will give you a very good hiding."

"I am not your kid. I am not scared of you!" I shot back, to the astonishment of the other new students. But inside, I was almost wetting myself. Warlord walked away.

The head teacher welcomed us to the school at the first assembly in the school hall. He advised us new students to befriend the senior students and learn the norms and values of the school. My intestines turned.

The threats of Warlord tormented my mind during the first lessons. I barely paid any attention. After lessons, I tried phoning my dad, but the line was engaged. I tried phoning my mum but her mobile phone was switched off. I felt alone and helpless. When I returned to my room, Warlord and his gang were waiting for me.

"Withdraw your report to the boarding master," Warlord screamed at me. "Your roommate won't testify; we already sorted it out with him."

"I won't."

Warlord grabbed me by the throat and pinned my head against the wall. I screamed in pain. He let go of me.

"Bastard!" Warlord yelled at me.

I knelt by the bedside and reached for the knife under my mattress.

Warlord's eyes popped out when he saw what was in my hand. I charged at him.

Warlord cowered to a corner of the room. His gang members bolted. I waved the glinting knife in Warlord's face like a mad man. "Who is the coward now?"

Suddenly, Mr Dondo burst into the room. "Simbarashe, put down the knife!"

I dropped the knife.

***

My best laid plan had failed. I had loathed swapping the bright lights of Harare for some remote boarding school in Buhera, so I stole my mother's kitchen knife. I was never going to stab Warlord. I only meant to scare him, but ideally, I wanted to be expelled from the boarding school. Instead, I got away with a caution for bringing a kitchen knife into the boarding school.

Prisoner of Conscience

The prison van pulled into Salisbury Central prison car park. My teeth chattered. Handcuffs fastened my wrists like a vice grip. A cold chill nipped into my body at the back of the prison van. I peeked through the meshed wire windows of the van. The rays of the morning sun danced on the white prison walls which had tall fences and sharp spikes. I had a sinking feeling. The engine of the prison van died down. My hair stood on its edges.

A black prison officer opened the front door of the van and jumped out. He strode to the back and unlocked the door which creaked as he swung it open. "Get out!"

I jumped out. Blood clogged my veins.

The officer grabbed my arm and marched me to the entrance of the prison. The inside was designed like a panopticon. He led me down a long corridor to a small office. There, he handed a piece of paper to a short, stern white prison warden, who held a baton stick.

The warden read the piece of paper then glared at me. "So, you are a terrorist, boy?" There was a cynical smile on his face.

"I'm not a terrorist. I'm a freedom fighter."

"Whose freedom are you fighting for?"

"The black majority."

"Don't talk back to me, boy!" The warden hissed. His bulging eyes were gawking at me.

"I'm not your boy."

"Shut up, you black bastard!" His face turned red. His mouth frothed with saliva. "In here, I will re-educate you, boy. I have turned communists and terrorists like you into law-abiding natives."

"I said, I am not your boy." I looked at him defiantly.

"You bloody black bastard!" The warden whacked me hard on the nose with his baton stick. He spit into my face.

Pain shot up my eyeballs to my brain. I winced. Blood dripped down my nostrils, staining my white T-shirt.

"Get this bastard out of my sight!" He barked at one of the black prison wardens. "Lock him up in the dungeon." I felt angry, helpless and terrified.

The black prison warden led me to a small toilet. There, he took off my handcuffs and handed me tissues. "Stop the bleeding from your nose."

When I pressed my nose with the tissue, I smelt blood.

"Take off your clothes."

I took off my stained T-shirt, jeans, socks, coins, wristwatch, wallet and tennis shoes. I handed the things to him.

He shoved them into a dirty sack. He handed me a white prison shirt and a pair of shorts. "Put these on."

I obliged. I felt awkward.

The warden handed me two blankets and a mat. "Follow me." I lumbered behind him.

The prison warden stopped outside cell 16. He unlocked the heavy, squeaking metal door. "Welcome to the dungeon." My knees trembled. I hesitated. The warden pushed me into the dark, windowless cell. Immediately, he slammed shut the metal door.

My heart jumped out of my rib cage. I looked around the cell after my eyes had adjusted to the darkness. It was filthy and smelt like a public lavatory. I shuffled around the cold floor, feeling like a trapped mouse. The words '**Stay in the struggle**' were written in bold, black letters, on the grey walls of the cell.

I rolled out the small mat onto the cold floor and spread one blanket over it. I folded the other blanket into a pillow and lay down. My nose was aching. A small bucket with a fetid smell in the corner of the cell was my toilet. The dirty blankets were itchy and smelly. I scratched all over my body now developing pimples.

I closed my eyes and thought about Ruth, my wife, my mother, and my father. Tears flooded my eyes when I recounted the heated conversation I had had with my father.

***

"Why are you getting involved in black nationalist politics?" My father raised his voice, fastening his eyes onto me. "Tell me why, Edson! I struggled so I could send you to the University of Rhodesia. You have a good teaching job. Why black nationalist politics? Do you want to be detained by the Rhodesian police?"

I cleared my throat. "Father, look at the racial discrimination at University of Rhodesia. One hundred and fifty black students were expelled for demonstrating against racial discrimination on campus. Look at the political repression. Black nationalist leaders are either dead, in detention or exile. Now is the time to revolt against this repressive, white colonial regime."

"Listen, Edson. I'm not interested in any of that. It doesn't put *sadza* on my table."

"Father, I am grateful that you worked hard to send me to university," I said, looking directly at him. "But what is the value of education without freedom? Look at Ghana and Nigeria. They are enjoying black majority rule. They are independent nations. We need that independence and freedom here in Rhodesia."

"Good for them. Our time for independence will come."

"How will it come? Independence will not come without a fight. It will not be handed to us on a silver plate. We must fight for it. We must fight against the repression, the mass unemployment and the poverty in black townships."

"Well, my son," my father concluded, "you are a man. You must bear the consequences of your actions. A man who swallows a bone is proud of his anus." My father stood up and walked away.

After the conversation, I became even more emboldened as an activist for black nationalism. I soon moved out of the family home to a rented four-roomed house with my newlywed wife, Ruth.

***

The jangling of keys as someone unlocked the heavy cell door interrupted my reverie. The door swung open. Light and fresh air flooded into the dark, dank cell. A black prison warden stepped in and placed a plate of food and a spoon on the dirty floor.

"What have you brought me?"

The prison warden did not reply. He slammed shut the metal door, locked it and walked away.

I was hungry and slurped up the porridge. My eyes were heavy with sleep. I recalled the raid.

***

The hard knock on the front door woke me with a start. Heavy boots pounded the ground outside.

Who is outside my house at midnight? I jumped out of bed and tiptoed through the darkness of the bedroom to the lounge. I peeked through a lace curtain.

Outside, armed Rhodesian police officers, *majoni*, were everywhere. Two police cars and a van beamed their head lights, illuminating the house. I trembled. There was a loud bang on the front door. I mustered some courage. "Who is it?"

"Rhodesian police! Open up!" Bellowed a voice from outside the housc.

"What do you want?"

"We have a warrant to search your house."

"Search for what?" My body was drenched in sweat.

"Open the door!"

"Show me your police badge on the window."

"Don't waste my time, boy!" I peeped through the window and saw the shining police badge. Adrenalin flooded my veins.

"Alright. Give me two minutes to dress up."

"Chop! Chop! Hurry up!" The voice barked impatiently. I dashed back to the bedroom.

"What is going on, Edson?" Ruth asked, rubbing her sleepy eyes.

"Rhodesia police are here! It's a raid!" I quickly put on a pair of jeans, a white T-shirt and tennis shoes.

"Oh no, the papers! Where are they?" Ruth queried. I scoured through the wardrobe and found the papers.

"Hide them in the kitchen," I told Ruth.

Ruth rolled out of bed and dashed to the kitchen. I lifted the mattress and took a brown envelope from underneath it. I stuffed the envelope into my underwear. I rushed back to the lounge. There, I shoved the other papers under the cushion of a single sofa then switched on the lights.

"Open the door!" The voice bellowed. There was a loud banging on the door.

"Alright. I'm opening the door now." I exhaled and swung the door open.

A towering, fit white police officer wearing a grey shirt and khaki shorts stood on the doorstep, a baton stick in his hands. Behind him there were eight black police officers armed with AK47s, and a slim white female police officer. I froze.

"I am Chief Detective Flower," said the white police officer, the leader, bursting through the door.

"Why do you want to search my house?"

"Read the search warrant," he said, handing me a paper.

I read the warrant. "You must be kidding, right? You're searching for weapons and anti-government propaganda material?"

"Yes. We have intelligence stating that you have been recruiting guerrilla fighters, writing and distributing subversive anti-government propaganda material, and organising secret meetings to incite civil disobedience by the natives," Chief Detective Flower elucidated.

"You won't find any weapons in my house."

He ignored me. Instead, he turned to the black police officers. "Search every inch of this house." The officers nodded and dashed to the main bedroom.

"What is going on, Edson?" Ruth quizzed, coming out of the bedroom and feigning shock. I shrugged.

"You, shut up!" Chief Detective Flower squealed at Ruth.

Ruth wilted like a golden daffodil. Chief Detective Flower eyed me and growled some orders to a black officer, "Watch him."

"Yes sir," replied the officer. I screwed my face.

Chief Detective Flower turned to the female police officer, "Watch Miss Big Mouth here." He meant Ruth. The officer nodded.

The black police officers turned over the mattress and rummaged through the wardrobe. They emptied suitcases and laundry baskets. They found nothing. I sighed.

Chief Detective Flower followed the officers into the second bedroom. The officers ransacked the room. There was nothing there as well. I exhaled. Then the officers entered the kitchen and started clattering pots, pans, cups, and teapots in the kitchen unit. My intestines tightened. I was knock-kneed and sat down on the single sofa.

The black officer, my guard, hawk-eyed me like a chicken. I fiddled with my fingers. My heart juddered. Sweat dripped down my face.

"I've found something!" One of the black police officers yelled, triumphantly. He entered the lounge, holding a teapot with papers stuffed inside. "Sir, you should look at this," he said with a wide grin on his face. He handed the papers to Chief Detective Flower. I melted like ice.

Chief Detective Flower read the papers then smiled. "Good work, officer. Continue the search."

I deflated like a punctured tire.

The officers moved into the lounge. They sifted through the bookshelf and set aside two books: *Pedagogy of the Oppressed* by Paulo Freire and *Coming of the dry season* by Charles Mungoshi.

"Why are you reading these banned books?" Chief Detective Flower interrogated me. His face was deformed by anger.

"I read what I want, when I want," I said. Chief Detective Flower gaped his mouth. My heart palpitated as the officers searched closer to the sofa.

"Look under the cushion of the sofa," Chief Detective Flower ordered one of the black officers. I remained seated.

"Stand up, boy!" Chief Detective Flower bawled at me. I trembled and hesitated, then slowly stood up. The black officer lifted the cushion off the single sofa. Immediately, he saw the papers. He picked them up and read them before he handed them to Chief Detective Flower. My mind wallowed in dread.

"Handcuff him. Bring him to the charge office for further interrogation!" Chief Detective Flower declared with elation. Tears glistened in my eyes as I was handcuffed.

"I love you, Edson." Ruth hugged me.

"I love you too, Ruth." I kissed her on the cheek. A lump blocked my oesophagus.

Two black officers pulled me away.

"Find me a solicitor as soon as possible!" I yelled to Ruth as I was led away to a police van parked in the driveway.

The neighbours on Musasa road gazed at the unfolding drama with disbelief. The flashing lights, banging doors, the noise, drones of police vehicles and the commotion had awoken them. I was whisked away into the night.

***

The officers paraded me from the entrance of Salisbury Police Charge Office to a small office at the end of the corridor. The office had a notice on the door, **For Native Police Officers**.

Five black officers were typing documents inside the muggy office. It was crammed with desks, dirty files, and filing cabinets and I felt claustrophobic as I sat on a hard, wooden bench. A black police officer guarded me.

The busy police officers momentarily lifted their eyes from their typewriters, gazing at me. I looked away.

"Can I please use the toilet?" I asked the officer guarding me.

"Alright. But be quick about it." He led me to a small toilet with a notice on the door, **For Natives Only**.

Inside the toilet cubicle, I took out the brown envelope that I had shoved into my underwear during the raid. I opened it. Inside, there was a piece of paper listing names of young men I had recruited to join the war of liberation. I tore up the envelope and the list and flushed the shreds of paper down the toilet. I felt relieved.

The police officer, my guard, led me back to the small office.

"Sit quiet while the officers are typing your charge sheet!" Ordered the police officer. I obliged.

Eventually, I was led away by my guard to a spacious, brightly lit, well-ventilated office. He took off my handcuffs. Chief Detective Flower sat behind a desk in the office. "Sit down!" He ordered me, pointing to an empty chair. I sat down.

"We have uncovered plenty of evidence from your house showing that you have been terribly busy writing and distributing anti-government propaganda material and organising secret meetings." Chief Detective Flower prattled. "Now, read this detention order and sign it." He handed me the detention order.

I read it. "I won't sign it! I know my rights." I protested, shaking my head.

"You're being detained for violating the Law-and-Order Act 1960," declared Chief Detective Flower.

"You can't detain me for exercising my civil rights in my country," I protested.

"Your so-called 'black nationalist activities' are banned under the Law-and-Order Maintenance Act 1960," Chief Detective Flower reiterated, with his eyes widening. "Now sign the detention order. Or else I will add charges on your wife, Ruth. She was aiding and abetting your activities."

"Leave Ruth out of this!"

"Sign the detention order."

"Ruth is innocent."

"Are you the guilty one?"

"No."

"Sign the detention order." Chief Detective Flower shrieked.

"I won't sign the detention order without my solicitor being present."

Chief Detective Flower laughed scornfully. "I'll use the emergency powers anyway, to detain you without your solicitor present."

I was flabbergasted.

"Sign the order!" Chief Detective Flower screamed, banging the desktop.

I was rattled. Eventually, I signed the detention order. My admission of guilt, under duress, spared Ruth from further harassment by the Rhodesian police. Chief Detective Flower giggled as I was led away to a waiting prison van.

***

Ruth came to visit me in Salisbury prison. Her countenance was bright white and angelic. She wafted on clouds like an angel.

"Thank you for coming so soon," I said.

"I missed you, Edson."

"I missed you too, Ruth." A black prison warden hovered above Ruth and me like an eagle. An uneasiness pervaded our reunion.

"How is mother and father?" I asked.

"Fine."

"How are you?"

"Fine. And you?" Ruth's eyes glowed like gems.

"I'm holding up well." I feigned a smile. Tears glistened in Ruth's eyes. She looked away.

"Have you found me a solicitor?"

"Yes," Ruth replied.

"That's good news!" I beamed. I reached out to kiss her.

Suddenly, I woke up from the dream. My body was drenched in sweat. My mind jolted back to reality. I looked around the prison cell. It was deathly silent. For a fleeting moment, my mind had drifted away in the arms of Morpheus. I had a vision of a candle flame of hope burning bright inside the dark cell. I prayed that the flame would continue to burn bright inside my soul, inside my mind, inside the desolate confines of the prison cell.

The Promised Land

John Smith is sitting with his family in the kitchen, eating breakfast, when three Toyota Hilux 4X4 trucks, two red and one white, pull up into the car park at their Homewood farmhouse.

Smith, or Baas John as his farm workers know him, is unsettled by the sight of strangers pulling up at his farm unannounced. After all, these are not ordinary times, with all the talk of evicting white settlers from their farms. Wiping his mouth, he stands up, walks slowly to the dining room window, and peers outside.

Ten sturdy and stern-looking black men exit the three trucks. Three of the men are armed with rifles. Baas John's heart misses a pulse.

"Who are they, John?" Asks Rebecca, his wife, an elegant woman whose radiant beauty belies her forty-five years. She is still seated at the dining room table with their two sons, James and Robert.

"I don't know these men. I better go out and see what they want," says Baas John, snatching his AK47 rifle. Trembling, he opens the door.

Tightly clutching the rifle in his shaking hands, Baas John approaches the visitors. His eagle eyes are fixed on them. "Good morning, gentlemen. What brings you to Homewood farm?"

A short, dark man with a waist like a baobab tree stump steps forward. He is wearing a safari suit and appears to be the leader of the group. "I am Comrade Tichatonga, a war veteran, and these are my comrades," he says, pointing at the other men. Peering directly into Baas John's eyes, Comrade Tichatonga begins to speak authoritatively. "I am here to notify you that as of today, I own Homewood farm. It has been acquired by the government under the Land Redistribution Program and offered to me as a war veteran." He hands a typewritten piece of paper to Baas John.

Baas John reads it then angrily tosses it back to Comrade Tichatonga. "What is this nonsense? I hold the title deeds to Homewood farm."

Comrade Tichatonga picks up the paper from the dusty ground. His big eyeballs inflate with anger. "Now listen here, white man," he fumes, pointing his finger at Baas John. "I want you off my land in twenty-four hours."

"Bullshit!" Barks Baas John. "This farm has belonged to my family for three generations. I am not giving it up."

Comrade Tichatonga gapes his mouth in disbelief. Then with emphasis, he retorts, "This land rightfully belongs to our ancestors who were forcibly removed by yours. Now we want our land back."

Baas John's jaw drops. "I may be white, but I am an African, born and bred on this farm. How can you say I no longer own this farm? Be warned, you gentlemen are trespassing on private property."

Comrade Tichatonga and his men laugh sarcastically. "This land belongs to the indigenous black people of this country, the landless peasants whose rights your ancestors took away."

Baas John laughs disdainfully. "So, you gentlemen are the landless peasants? Since when do poor, landless peasants drive posh Toyota Hilux 4X4 twin cabs?" Comrade Tichatonga frowns. The other men are incensed by the remark and want to charge at Baas John, but he dissuades them with a hand signal.

"It is none of your business what cars we drive. You have twenty-four hours to vacate this farm. This is our promised land and we are going to take it back."

"What do you mean by our promised land?"

"This land was promised to us by the ruling party as compensation for our sacrifices in liberating this country." Balls of sweat emerge on Comrade Tichatonga's forehead.

"Well, my land is not your promised land, and neither is it up for acquisition. Go back to whoever sent you and tell them that."

"Alright then, white man, we have served you the ultimatum," Comrade Tichatonga declares finally. "We will be back. You should be gone by then or else be prepared to face the consequences."

Comrade Tichatonga and his men turn and briskly walk back to their trucks and speed off.

Shocked by what has just transpired, Baas John remains transfixed as he watches the cars disappear in clouds of dust. He ponders over the threats from Comrade Tichatonga.

"John, what did those men want?" Rebecca asks him when he gets back to the house. Her face is pale and she can see that her husband is shaken. Baas John drops into his chair. "Would you believe it? The so-called war veterans have just driven up and tried to throw me off my land. They want me out in twenty-four hours, but I am not going anywhere. My grandfather acquired this farm eighty years ago under the Land Apportionment Act of 1930."

Robert turns his candid ten-year-old gaze on his father and asks, "Who owned the land before that?" Rebecca and James cast sharp, angry looks at him. He looks away.

"The native Shona people lived on the land before the white minority government moved them in the 1930s to the reserves to make way for white commercial farms," explains Baas John.

"Oh," mutters Robert. Baas John finishes breakfast in a quiet, sullen mood. He goes out for his daily briefings with the farm manager and workers. That afternoon, right after the lunch break, Baas John gathers all the workers inside the large farm barn.

"This morning," begins Baas John, his voice trembling and his face etched with fear, "Comrade Tichatonga, a man who claims to be a war veteran, came by and gave me an ultimatum to vacate the farm in twenty-four hours." There are murmurs of shock from the hundred or so farm workers sitting crammed on the dirty cement floor of the barn.

Sibanda, the head of security at Homewood farm, a giraffe of a man, asks, "Baas John, what are we going to do?"

Baas John clears his throat. "The farm is the source of our livelihood. We have no option but to defend it. We must or else our whole lives' work turns to dust."

"How are we going to defend the farm from those marauding war veterans?" Asks one farm worker.

"I will supply every able-bodied man with a rifle and ammunition," replies Baas John.

His words are greeted with contemplative silence by the group who know that the war veterans are ruthless with black farm workers seen to be siding with white farmers.

"How about a negotiated settlement with the war veterans?" Asks Sibanda.

"There is no way I am negotiating with that thief!" Bass John screams as he turns his glowering eyes to Sibanda. "On whose side are you now, Sibanda? Mine? Or the war veterans?"

"Your side, Baas." Sibanda quickly reassures his boss. "You have been kind to us on the farm over the years; we will stand by you, Baas."

The other farm workers clap their hands, cheer, and whistle in approval. The meeting soon adjourns, and the workers return to the fields.

Bass John asks Sibanda and a few of his men to remain behind. He wants to hear more about Comrade Tichatonga. The man, he learns, has the full support of the ruling party and is one of the men spearheading the invasion of white settler owned commercial farms in the whole district.

For many years, Bass John had owned and managed Homewood farm, developing it into a successful commercial venture, earning him foreign currency through the export of maize, tobacco, flowers and fruits to the European Union. Now the Supreme Court of the country had ruled that his land must be redistributed to redress the wrongs of the Land Apportionment Act of 1930. This court ruling had sparked the wave of land invasions by the likes of Comrade Tichatonga.

The following day, Baas John wakes up at dawn and organises his men to mend the fences and securely barricade all gates into Homewood farm. By dusk, Bass John and his men are exhausted. The fear of losing his cherished farm eats away at him. He sits on the veranda of the farmhouse, seeping Mazoe raspberry squash and peering at the weary, orange sun lying on the bed of the horizon. Dark, pregnant clouds hover over the sub-Saharan sky.

Suddenly, Baas John hears loud singing and the drones of vehicles in the distance. Plumes of dust rise on the horizon and a procession of lorries, pickup trucks and twin cabs approach Homewood farm, crammed full of youths chanting revolutionary songs at the top of their voices. Baas John rushes into the dining room and watches the scene from the window. The procession stops outside the main gate. Comrade Tichatonga jumps out of his twin cab and tries to open the gate, but it is locked. He furiously clinks the chains on the gate.

The men dismount from the backs of the vehicles. Many are wearing ruling party t-shirts and waving placards written, "This country will never be a colony again." The mob is heavily armed with machetes, axes, sticks and rifles.

Baas John trembles at the sight of the menacing, wild mob. The only protection between him and their rage are the two securely bolted gates into the farm. He hears Comrade Tichatonga addressing the mob on his loudspeaker. "My fellow comrades, the white man has locked us out of our land. What a cheeky white man! Today we will show him we mean business."

Wild cheers of approval erupt from the frenzied mob. Comrade Tichatonga leads the mob as they continue chanting slogans and singing revolutionary songs.

Meanwhile, inside the dining room, Baas John is pacing and scratching his head. The reality of the siege makes him feel vulnerable and insecure.

Rebecca, unhinged by fear, huddles on the couch with James and Robert. She momentarily smothers a tear. "John, what are we going to do?" She asks in a petrified tone.

Baas John stops and switches on the dining room lights. "You and the boys must start packing your valuables. Get ready to leave."

"How are we going to get past those barbarians?" Rebecca asks in disbelief.

"When it is darker, you, the boys, the farm driver and five of the guards will exit the farm through the back gate. I will stay behind with the rest of the guards and try to disperse the mob," replies Baas John.

"That is extremely dangerous, John. If this place is not safe for me and the boys, it is not safe for you either."

"Rebecca, this is not the time for arguments," declares Baas John.

Rebecca stands up. "You have to be careful John. I don't want to be widowed at forty-five and I don't plan to raise the boys without a father."

Baas John turns to his children. "I guess you boys should go and help your mum pack," he says calmly. Inside, his heart melts.

The two boys quietly stand up and head to the main bedroom.

Now alone, Baas John listens to the sonorous singing and drum beats from the main gate. His blood seethes.

An hour later, Baas John walks out of the farmhouse. It is now pitch dark. The mob outside the gate has stopped singing. He can see them cooking and chatting around fires. He hurries back into the house. Turning to Rebecca and the boys, he says, "You must leave now, while the invaders are distracted."

Baas John quickly kisses and hugs James and Robert. He turns to Rebecca, hands her a rifle and gives final instructions. "This rifle is loaded. Make sure your hand is always on the trigger and shoot if anyone tries to attack you. Here are the keys to the back gate. Check into a motel. I will join you soon."

"John, please be careful against those thugs," pleads Rebecca. She kisses her husband and hugs him tightly.

Baas John leads his family to the pickup truck waiting outside. Five guards armed with rifles carry four packed suitcases and jump onto the back of the truck. Sadness overwhelms Bass John when the farm driver starts the truck. He waves at his family.

Back inside the dining room, Baas John briefs the farm guards who have congregated there. "Remember, our goal is to disperse these invaders. My group will target the mob at the main gate. Sibanda and his group will go after the looters in the maize fields and orchard. Let us stay close to each other." He hands out twenty rifles and rubber bullets to the guards. The farm guards pensively load their rifles.

Then stealthily, Baas John and Sibanda lead their two groups out of the farmhouse. They creep towards the invaders. The blanket of darkness provides good cover.

As Baas John and his men creep closer, the mob starts singing and dancing around the bonfires, unaware of the impending threat. Adrenaline courses through Baas John's body. He exhales. He wipes away sweat from his forehead. Through the illumination of the fire, he can see that only three of the men in the mob appear to be armed with rifles. The rest are wielding sticks, machetes, and metal bars. He motions to his men to stop. He aims his rifle at the mob and counts to three with his fingers.

Suddenly, the staccato of gunfire reverberates. A startled Comrade Tichatonga is hit, stumbles and falls. He gets up, runs for cover inside his twin cab and drives off. The mob scurries away from the gate like rodents. Baas John and the farm guards continue firing after the fleeing mob.

Another volley of gunfire from Sibanda and his group pierces the tranquil night from the maize fields and orchards. After a while, the firing stops. Only the noises of the fleeing farm invaders can be heard in the distance.

“Good job guys,” Baas John commends his guards. Baas John and his men return to the farmhouse. There is an eerie silence and cold breeze wafting in the night. The guards take turns to patrol the farm. Some of them go to guard the workers’ compounds.

Baas John throws himself on the couch, clutching his rifle in his arms. He worries what will happen if the farm invaders return with reinforcements. *Would he be able to dig in and defend his farm?* He falls asleep.

At midnight, there is a sudden heavy battering on the dining room door. Baas John wakes with a start and scrambles to his feet, clutching his rifle. His legs are numb with fear. The farm guards who had dozed off on the dining room floor, leaped up, dreary eyed, with their rifles pointed towards the door.

“Who is it?” Bass John asks.

“Please Baas John, open quickly. It is Sibanda,” mutters a terrified voice from outside.

Baas John heaves a sigh of relief. “What is the matter, Sibanda?”

Out of breath and trembling, Sibanda stumbles into the dining room muttering, “The farm invaders have returned, Baas. They cut the locks on the main gate, overran the worker’s compound and are rounding up and beating the workers and their families. They are heading this way and this time, they are well-armed.”

A cold sensation runs down Baas John’s spine. His hair stands up and adrenalin sends him into fight mode. He rushes to the gun cabinet, snatches his sub-machine gun and loads it. He hands out small boxes of live rounds to the guards.

“Baas, I think we should leave before the farm invaders arrive,” pleads Sibanda.

Baas John shakes his head. “That bastard Comrade Tichatonga and his thugs will pay for trespassing on my farm.” He is drunk with rage.

Baas John, Sibanda and the farm guards rush out of the farmhouse onto the veranda. Guns are pointed in all directions. They see an angry, rowdy mob marching towards them, up the driveway wielding torches, axes and machetes.

Baas John orders the guards to open fire. He squeezes the trigger of his submachine gun. A loud burst of gunfire erupts. Several bodies in the mob drop to the ground like sacks. There are loud screams. The mob disperses and takes cover behind the barn. They curse loudly and start hauling stones and firebombs at the farmhouse. Some stones shatter the glass on the dining room windows. Baas John and the guards dodge the flying missiles and return live fire towards the barn.

Suddenly, a powerful bust of machine gunfire booms from behind the barn. The bullets narrowly miss Baas John and his men.

In the hail of bullets, Baas John dashes for his pickup truck in the car pack. A bullet whizzes past his ear. He jumps into the truck and starts the engine, screaming to his guards, "Get in! Get in!"

The farm guards dash for the pickup truck whilst firing at the barn and jump into the back. Heavy machine gun fire shutters the windscreen.

The pickup truck whisks off. Through the rear-view mirror, Baas John sees the farm invaders torching the farmhouse. His heart melts, but the thought of his family safe in a motel, far from the mad mob soothes him.

The Miser and the Golden Leaf

Although Jambwa was a prosperous farmer of the tobacco crop, the popular golden leaf, he had a notorious reputation as a miser. He kept for himself most of the profits from the sale of the crop while paying his farm workers a pittance. Sometimes Jambwa did not even pay his labourers at all. He withdrew the festive season presents that the farm workers had been accustomed to receiving from the previous white farmer at the end of each year.

Jambwa had acquired the 30 000-hectare Chitomborwizi commercial farm by evicting a white commercial farmer at the height of the violent land redistribution programme. Despite his notoriety, Jambwa was never short of cheap farm labourers queuing to find work on his farm, planting tobacco, spraying pesticides, harvesting, and curing the tobacco and loading bales for the auction floors.

Something attracted the farm labourers to Jambwa's farm. Even the old farm labourers were not keen on leaving, despite the neighbouring farms paying better wages.

***

One day, Jambwa and the farm foreman, Mujubeki, were sitting on garden chairs on the veranda of the farmhouse. The two men, thirsty from the heat of the day, were drinking cold water from glasses and peering at the orange sun disappearing on the bed of the horizon. It was the crack of dusk on a baking day. The air was dense and dry.

Jambwa gulped down water from his glass and put it on the garden table. He planted a broad smile on his dark, oval face and said, "The golden leaf has earned me a fortune on the auction floors this season." The smile revealed his pearly white teeth. He peered through the paper showing the Profit and Loss Accounts.

"That is pleasing news," replied Mujubeki shrewdly. He took a sip of water and he looked at the net profit on the accounts.

"I am more successful than the previous white farmer," boasted Jambwa.

Mujubeki nodded his head. Then, fixing his big, searching eyes on Jambwa, he quizzed, "Does this mean you will raise the pay of the workers? It has been five years since the last one."

Jambwa frowned. He cleared his throat and remarked, "I am afraid there is no money left for a pay increase when I have paid off all the expenses on seeds, pesticides, water, electricity, transport and the Agribank loan."

Mujubeki gazed at Jambwa with a cynical look. "But you have just said that you had a profitable tobacco farming season. Besides, we deserve some appreciation for our hard work in the fields. Without us, the farming season would not have been as successful."

Jambwa shook his head. "A pay increase is a privilege I am not prepared to offer at this juncture. Maybe next season if there is a bumper harvest."

"A pay increase is a right not a privilege," declared Mujubeki. "The farm workers do not have the patience to wait till next season."

"Are you planning on ganging up with the farm workers to riot on my farm?" Jambwa raising his voice.

"No, Baas. I am only stating the obvious. Give us a fair wage for losing our skins in the sweltering heat of the fields."

Jambwa stood up. "Now, go and tell the farm labourers," he boldly declared with his big eyeballs fixed on Mujubeki, "that they either put up with the current wage or pack their bags and leave my farm." He sat down.

Mujubeki angrily rose from his chair and briskly walked away without uttering a word.

Jambwa remained seated, gazing at Mujubeki disappearing into the darkening day, seething with anger.

Early the following morning, Jambwa visited the tobacco fields. It was a chilly morning. As he approached the fields on his bicycle, Jambwa sounded its bell to announce his arrival. The farm labourers dispersed from a gathering they were having and scrambled back to harvesting the tobacco leaves.

Jambwa dismounted and looked around suspiciously. He walked over to Mujubeki. "I have come to inform you that with effect from today, I am extending the working day by an extra hour to 6pm. I must sell the remaining tobacco in the fields before the auction floors close."

"But we still have not resolved the pay issue," Mujubeki protested.

"I will offer you a token reward instead of a pay increase for your hard work," said Jambwa nonchalantly "Meanwhile, it is better to work hard and harvest the remaining tobacco leaves than spend precious time on fruitless wage demands."

Mujubeki did not reply. He quietly went back to work. Jambwa jumped back onto his bicycle and rode off.

Mujubeki gathered the farm labourers and addressed them. "Since Jambwa is unwilling to give us a pay rise, we should make him pay for his stubbornness, continue working in the fields as if nothing has happened. No one should tell Jambwa what we have just discovered."

All the farm labourers agreed to seal their mouths. The extended working hour was a blessing in disguise; they had more time for their covert work in the fields under the disguise of harvesting tobacco.

Jambwa was content with the subservience of his farm labourers. He loved the power he wielded when putting them in their rightful place. However, to his annoyance, the meaner he grew towards his farm labourers, the more they seemed unfazed. This bothered him.

In contrast, Mujubeki's popularity among the farm labourers grew. As the end of tobacco auction season drew closer, Jambwa's ego grew bigger as his bank account grew fatter. He did not pay the bonus as he had promised. But eventually, nagged by a sense of guilt and wanting to gain favour with the farm workers, Jambwa proposed to offer the farm labourers a reward of a five-kilogram bag of maize meal every month.

The farm labourers flatly refused the token offer. They demanded a proper pay rise. Jambwa was unwilling to compromise.

Mujubeki and the farm workers stopped asking for a pay increase and instead became more preoccupied with working the tobacco fields.

Jambwa's curiosity was soon aroused by their suspicious behaviour. Whenever he visited the tobacco fields, the farm workers would whistle loudly to each other and scramble back to work. The daily tobacco harvest targets were not being met.

Mujubeki said the farm labourers were disgruntled over the low pay.

Despite the poor wages that Jambwa paid, the farm workers still managed to send their children to school. On Sunday, the day off, the farm workers dressed smartly in expensive clothes and drank beer heavily without a care in the world.

Jambwa began his investigation. He inspected the tobacco fields on a Sunday afternoon, and he discovered the topsoil in the tobacco fields had been dug up and then put back. "Probably the hungry farm labourers were digging for mice," thought Jambwa.

On a cloudy, late Sunday afternoon, Jambwa decided to spy on the farm labourers at their residential compound. When Jambwa got closer to the compound, he crawled and hid behind a bush, observing the activity in the compound from a distance.

After a while, an expensive, sleek Mercedes Benz pulled up. The driver remained in his car. Jambwa had never seen the car before. Mujubeki walked up to the Mercedes Benz holding something wrapped in aluminium foil. He leaned his head through the open window and handed the wrapped parcel to the driver. The car driver handed Mujubeki a bulging khaki envelope and quickly drove off. The farm labourers quickly surrounded Mujubeki. He began to hand out something which, even from that distance, Jambwa could see, were dollar bills.

After the commotion, the farm workers began to ululate, jive to the loud music of Macheso and drink beer.

Jambwa grew more suspicious. Who was the driver of Mercedes Benz? What was he doing on his farm? He stealthily crawled away from the bush and returned to the farmhouse. He waited for the cover of darkness to investigate the suspicious activity going on in the workers' compound.

At nightfall, Jambwa put on torn black overalls, black gumboots and a black sun hat to cover his face. He disguised himself as a farm labourer. Then he staggered towards the compound like a drunk returning from a party.

Inside the workers' compound, the men and women were now reeling around in drunken jubilation and stupor, jiving to the blurring music of Macheso on the radiogram. No one noticed Jambwa entering the compound. Jambwa's heart started to beat hard as he staggered to a darkened spot at the edge of a hut. Mujubeki was in the centre of the crowd, bum-jiving to the music.

VaGaramukanwa, an old farm labourer, barely noticed Jambwa sit down on a stool half a metre from him. The old man was tipsy, and his eyes were glued to the festivities. The old man bobbed his head up and down, falling in and out of his drunken stupor. Silence pervaded the place when the music stopped playing.

Jambwa patted VaGaramukanwa on the shoulder and, speaking in a drunk and disguised tone, remarked, "Great party. What is the cause of celebration?"

"This is our farewell party. We are celebrating our final week working as slaves on this wretched farm," muttered VaGaramukanwa. He swigged a pint of beer.

"So where are you going then?" Jambwa quizzed.

"We have bought ourselves a farm in the district. We will be moving there at the end of this week," replied VaGaramukanwa wiping his frothy mouth with a handkerchief. Jambwa almost lost his temper.

But he kept his composure to maintain his cover. He probed further in his fake voice, "So where did you get the money to buy a farm?"

"When, by chance, we discovered gold deposits on the topsoil of the tobacco fields, we decided not to tell Jambwa," VaGaramukanwa revealed, "so, we have been extracting the gold deposits from the tobacco fields and covering the topsoil. Jambwa thinks we are harvesting his golden leaf. We have been selling the gold deposits to a buyer. Now that we have extracted all of the gold deposits, we are leaving Jambwa, the miser and his golden leaf."

Jambwa was dumbfounded and stood up, retreating to a darker edge of the hut. He leaned on the wall of the hut gasping for air. He felt excruciating pain in his chest, and he fell headlong, convulsing on the ground.

Suddenly, Thomas Mapfumo's song, *Ndavakuenda Ini*, began blaring on the radiogram and all the farm workers stood up to dance. The farm workers were too drunk to notice Jambwa's cold and lifeless body lying in the darkness of the hut. The wild party continued well into the night.

Lazarus rose from the dead

The news of Lazarus Chimbwido's sacking by his record label, Ghetto Boyz records, spread over social media platforms like a veld fire. Zim dancehall music fans were dying to know - why did Lazarus, also known as Ras Lazi, chanter of the popular tune, 'Kutsenga Waya', suddenly get dropped by his record label?

Different online versions of gossip spread regarding the sacking of Lazarus. Some fans suggested he had become too proud, leading to his downfall. Some posited that Lazarus had lost his way when he hooked up with his girlfriend, Pamela, a *slay queen* frequenting his music shows with other groupies. Others asserted that Lazarus had lost his vibe when he joined a notorious gang committing armed robberies in the city.

The simple truth was Lazarus had become addicted to cannabis and crystal meth, the latter known on Harare streets as *dombo* or *mutoriro*. On the fateful day of his sacking, Lazarus had staggered into the Ghetto Boyz Records studio, high as a parachute.

Godfather, Lazarus' record producer berated him, "Where have you been? You are two hours late for the recording session. Why didn't you answer your phone?"

"I was stuck in traffic in a commuter omnibus."

"Stuck in traffic? For two hours? Yeah, right. Traffic congestion in Harare of all places?"

"Yes."

"Enough is enough!" Godfather shook his head. "I warned you many times in the past about coming late for recording sessions because you're busy getting high on crystal meth and cannabis. But you just did not listen. You have twigs in your ears. Now, I have no other option but to drop you from my record label. You are now a liability to my business."

"You can't just drop me like that!" Lazarus argued in a slurred voice. He was almost falling forward in a stupor. His red eyes blinked intermittently. He reeked of cannabis.

"Yes, I can."

"What about our recording contract?"

"You breached the terms of the contract."

"How?"

"By showing up late and doing drugs."

"Nonsense!" Lazarus shook his head. "You still owe me royalties from Kutsenga Waya."

"I know that. I will pay you soon through Ecocash mobile money transfer. Goodbye, Lazarus." Godfather turned to two security guards who had biceps that bulged through their tight t-shirts. "Escort Lazarus out of the studio, please."

"You can't do this to me, Godfather," Lazarus protested as the security guards lifted him, even as he was vigorously kicking his legs. They dropped him outside the studio, in downtown Harare.

Lazarus got up, dusted himself and cursed the two guards who glared at him. They slammed the door of the studio on their way back in. Lazarus banged hard on the door, but no one opened. He eventually left, frustrated.

***

When Lazarus entered his girlfriend's flat, she was seething with anger. "What have you done, Lazarus? Godfather posted a YouTube video saying that you have been dropped from his record label. Why, Lazarus, why?"

"I don't know, Pamela. Godfather accused me of unprofessional conduct, saying I was turning up late for recording sessions, apparently high on cannabis and crystal meth. He is a parasite! He sucked me dry and now he has kicked me out of his studio onto the street." He sat on the sofa.

"Go back and apologise to him."

"Apologise? Me? Apologise to Godfather? That won't happen. There are many record producers in Harare."

"But Godfather and Ghetto Boyz are the best in the business."

"Maybe. Nevertheless, I am not going to apologise to Godfather."

"The problem with you, Lazarus, is pride. You are such a proud fool. Look, how you have fallen from grace because of it."

"Yeah, right. You call me a proud fool? What are you? A sensible *slay queen*?"

"Get out of my flat! How dare you call me a *slay queen*!"

"Alright." Lazarus stood up from the sofa and strolled into the bedroom. He started to pack his clothes into a duffle bag.

"Where do you think you are going?" Pamela asked him when she entered the bedroom.

"I am leaving."

"Where are you going?"

"To mum's. Didn't you just order me out of your flat?"

"Yes, I did. But I did not really mean it."

"But you said it. So, I am leaving."

"Stay, Lazarus. Please stay."

"No, I am leaving now."

"Okay, be my guest. Adios, amigo. Proud mama's boy, go on back to mama's apron strings. When will you learn to take responsibility for your mistakes?"

Lazarus glared at Pamela then continued packing his clothes. He flung the duffle bag over his shoulder and walked to the door. He turned to Pamela. "See you in another life, sensible Pamela." He gestured at her obscenely with two fingers and slammed the door on his way out.

***

Lazarus was happy back at his childhood home. He spent time reminiscing childhood memories. He immediately reunited with his former school friends for drug binges and catching up on the latest gossip and word on the streets.

Lazarus quickly became the toast of his friends and spent his meagre savings on buying crystal meth for them. His friends called him Mr Moneybags or *Mbinga.* Lazarus loved the label. He sunk deeper into his addiction.

Lazarus staggered home one day, at midnight. He opened the main door slowly, slipped inside the house and tiptoed past the lounge. He was halfway through when mum called him, "Lazarus, come here."

Mum was sitting on a sofa, shrouded in the darkness. Startled, Lazarus stood upright, straightened his shirt, and composed himself. He cleared his throat. Mum switched on the light. The abrupt, sharp light blinded him. He shielded his face with his hand and staggered to the sofa. Mum covered her nose from the strong smell of cannabis. "It is high time we talked, *mwanangu.*"

"What about?"

"I'm not happy seeing you spending so much time with your former schoolmates. I do not want you to end up like them - thieves, and drug addicts. Your father must be rolling inside his grave."

"They are my childhood friends, mum. I can't just disown them. But I will not end up like them."

"How can you play with a thief and not end up a thief? Those boys will milk you dry and then abandon you the moment you are penniless."

"I am a big boy, mum. I can take care of myself."

"You can succeed in your music career, but you lack discipline. I do not want you to die young." Mum choked and tears filled her eyes. She wiped away the tears with the palm of her hand.

Lazarus felt heartbroken, seeing his mum crying.

"I want you to live long, marry a decent woman from a decent family, and have children, my grandkids."

"I will get my mojo back. I will start a family when I find the right woman."

"Alright, my son. I just wanted you to know what is gnawing on my heart and mind. Good night."

"Good night, mum."

That night Lazarus could not sleep. He felt guilty that his misdemeanours had made mum shed tears. The image of mum crying stayed on his mind until he fell asleep.

***

Days later, Lazarus ran out of cash. But he was desperate for more drugs, so he pawned his black leather jacket.

That day, a new YouTube video was uploaded anonymously, saying that a former Zim dancehall music star had fallen on tough times and was resorting to selling his clothes to buy drugs.

Lazarus felt mortified that he had sunk so low that people were gossiping about him. He was angry and presumed that one of his close friends was the snitch who had ratted him out. He withdrew from his circle of friends because he did not know who to trust.

Lazarus' disappointment turned into depression as he struggled with withdrawal symptoms. He could no longer afford to buy drugs. He began to develop suicide ideation. None of his close friends came to see him or answered their phones when he attempted to phone them for some moral support during cold turkey. He locked himself in his bedroom for days.

Lazarus felt a near death experience as his body showed withdrawal symptoms. He staggered to the toilet every hour and green fluid came out of his mouth and anus. Pain hacked through his body. His sweat soaked the pillows. But through sheer grit, self-determination, and the support of mum, he eventually stopped taking the drugs.

One morning, mum knocked on Lazarus' bedroom door. "Rise and shine, Lazarus. Stop feeling sorry for yourself. I have a business proposal."

Lazarus woke up and dressed. He entered the lounge.

"Here is one hundred dollars. I want you to order and resell mobile phone top up cards. Please, do not buy drugs with the money. I will keep the profits for you until there is enough for recording sessions in a studio."

"Thanks, mum. I like the business proposal."

Lazarus took the money and went into town to order the mobile phone top up cards. The cards sold like hot cross buns, and he made a good profit. Lazarus fought the urge to buy drugs with the money. But he didn't give in to his urge. He returned home and handed the profits to mum.

Lazarus locked himself in his bedroom and began writing new songs. He sang the songs at dinner and mum was impressed by the songs. The new songs chronicled his struggle with drugs and kicking the addiction. He looked forward to the day he would stand behind a microphone inside a studio.

Another video surfaced on YouTube poking fun of Lazarus for falling on tough times and becoming a street vendor. Lazarus was furious and wanted to post his own YouTube video setting the record straight.

Mum dissuaded him, "Do not respond to those gossipers on social media platforms. All they ever do is peddle lies to gain more likes and views. Ignore them, Lazarus. Do not fall into their trap."

Lazarus took mum's advice. He grew more determined to prove his critics and detractors wrong.

But the following evening, Lazarus decided to post his own YouTube video instead, to his fans. In the tearful video, he said,

> "I am sincerely sorry to all ghetto youths and Zim dancehall fans that I let down. I struggled with an addiction to crystal meth and

cannabis, but now, I have beaten it. I am clean and ready to return to the studio. Again, I am sincerely sorry for letting everyone down due to my addiction.

I was upset by the fake news about me spreading on YouTube and other social media platforms from my critics and detractors. They danced on my grave like they did in bible times, on Lazarus'. But like my counterpart, I have risen from the dead. I got my mojo back and I have written new songs about my struggle and triumph over drug addiction.

Finally, I would like to express my sincere apologies to my mum, my girlfriend, Pamela, and my record producer, Godfather. I am sorry for the pain I caused you. I am appealing to Godfather and the other record producers in Harare to give me a second chance to resurrect my fledgling music career. I have learnt from my mistakes. A burnt child dreads fire.

Thanks, Big up!

This is yours, Lazarus, AKA Ras Lazi."

YouTube comments immediately started popping up. Many positive ones wished Lazarus well in his resurrected music career and urged him to remain clean and not relapse. A few negative comments labelled Lazarus "a loser who caused his own downfall." But Lazarus didn't mind them.

Later that evening, Lazarus was in the middle of penning new songs when his phone rang. His heart missed a beat when he saw the caller ID.

"Hi, Godfather. Long time. How have you been?"

"Fine. And you?"

"Good." There was a moment of silence.

"I called to commend you for the YouTube video that you posted tonight. You spoke candidly, from your heart. It was a stark reminder of the dangers of substance misuse. I am sincerely happy for you, for beating the addiction."

"Thanks."

"Can you pop by the studio tomorrow morning, to collect your royalties from Kutsenga Waya? We have a lot of catching up to do. I want to listen to your new songs."

"Thanks, Godfather. I cannot wait to see you tomorrow morning. Thanks."

"Good night."

Lazarus put his phone down. He jumped in the air and fist-pumped in jubilation. He couldn't wait to return to the booth in the studio and create new hit songs for his fans.

Scars of a Tree

An axe forgets that it hacked into a tree, but the tree remembers the blows of the axe and has deep scars to show.

-Shona proverb

The problems started after my mother died. I could not sleep and thought about her all the time. I did not know what to do. One night I fell asleep and saw my mother in a dream. She had wings and I nestled under them. When I woke up, I realised that I had wet the blankets. I was ashamed of myself.

"Why have you wet the blankets, Vongai?" My grandmother, VaMunyoro, berated me. Her sunken eyes bulged behind the thick lenses of her glasses. She shook her head with disgust.

"I don't know. One moment I was dreaming, the next, I woke up and saw that I had wet the blankets. I am sorry, Gogo. This will not happen again."

"It is shameful that a thirteen-year-old girl should be wetting her blankets. This must stop. You must try to be more hygienic. Take your blankets outside to dry."

I went outside and hung the blankets on the clothesline. I wished the earth would open and swallow me. That night, I had another dream. My mother took me by the hand and led me outside the hut to her grave. There, I talked to her for a while.

VaMunyoro came out, looking for me. She found me sitting on my mother's grave, at the edge of the village. "What are you doing here, alone? What has got into you, Vongai?"

I muttered something.

VaMunyoro shook me.

I slowly opened my eyes, blinking rapidly and confused.

"Tell me, Vongai? What has got into you?" VaMunyoro gazed at me from head to toe.

"I don't know."

"What do you mean, you don't know? An evil spirit has possessed you." VaMunyoro grabbed me by the neck and dragged me back to the hut.

Inside, she sat beside me, cogitating and staring into space. She was panting. The look on her face gave me the creeps. I fell asleep.

In the morning, I woke up and discovered that I had wet the blankets again. My mind was full of dread. VaMunyoro would devour me alive!

I overheard VaMunyoro speaking to two village women outside the hut. "I don't know what has got into her. She now wets the blankets every night. Guess where I found her last night? She was sitting on her mother's grave. An evil spirit has got into Vongai."

"Maybe she is struggling with the process of grieving. She should see a doctor at the hospital. It's not been long since she lost her mother," said one of the women.

"No, no. This has nothing to do with grieving," interjected the other woman. "This is a spiritual matter. Vongai is now possessed by the many evil spirits prowling this village. She should go and see Pastor Gumbo. He is a spiritual man of God. He will cast out the evil spirits possessing her."

"I don't know about that." VaMunyoro said. "I might have to take her to Pastor Gumbo for prayers if she continues bedwetting and sleepwalking. A spirit must be possessing her at night."

I waited until they had dispersed before going outside to hang my wet blankets.

That afternoon, I went to fetch water from the village borehole. As I approached the borehole, I overheard the two women who had been at my homestead earlier in the morning, gossiping. The women were washing their clothes at the borehole.

"Isn't it bizarre that a thirteen-year-old girl wets her blankets and walks in her sleep to her mother's grave at midnight?" one woman asked.

"Maybe she is a child witch," suggested the other woman.

"You are right. There has always been something dark in that girl's eyes."

"I don't want my children playing with her anymore."

I coughed. There was silence.

The two women shifted their gazes towards me. Their eyeballs almost popped out.

I was tongue tied. I cleared my throat. "Good afternoon."

"Good afternoon, Vongai," one woman replied, forcing a smile.

I pumped water from the borehole into my water bucket. I quietly walked away. *Why were they gossiping about me?* I thought. The two women stared at me until I was out of sight.

The following day, I went to the village borehole again. It was a hot afternoon. There, I saw a young girl drop her empty water bucket and bolt as I approached her. She stopped some distance away from me, clearly frightened, as if she had seen a ghost.

I glared at her. "Why are you running away?"

"Because you are a child witch," the young girl said.

"What! Who told you that lie?"

"My mother. She said you visit graves at night."

"I'm not a witch."

"Are you calling my mother a liar?"

"Yes."

"My mother also said you need deliverance from witchcraft," the young girl said.

My blood boiled. I felt dizzy. Tears poured out of my eyes. I pumped water from the borehole angrily and returned home, crying.

"I shouldn't have confided in those two gossipers," VaMunyoro said, after I had narrated the incident with the young girl at the borehole. "This gossiping must end. I will confront those two snakes before the gossip spreads like a wild bushfire throughout this village." She shook her head.

***

The lies spread. Some villagers said I was indeed a child witch and forbade their daughters from playing with me. I began to play alone at my homestead. The accusations made me feel sad because of how unfair they were. I was close to some of the village girls who were no longer allowed to play with me.

However, some villagers defended me, dismissing the child-witch lies and reasoning that I was an orphan who needed care and love instead. Their rationale was drowned by the loud lies.

The lies even spread to school. Other school children shunned me in class and on the playground at break times. The teachers heard what was going on, but they did not bother with village gossip.

I started missing school to avoid the name calling, the finger pointing and the shunning. I felt like it was my fault everyone was calling me a child witch. I wished I could die and be with my mother.

***

"It's about time you went to see Pastor Gumbo," VaMunyoro said one evening.

"What for?" I quizzed.

"For prayers."

"I don't need prayers."

"You do. Especially after those sleepless nights I had because of your sleepwalking and bedwetting."

“I wish you would listen to me just this once. I lost my mother, and I miss her a lot. I don’t need a spiritual healer. I need to see a doctor instead.”

“No, you don’t. You need Pastor Gumbo. I have heard a lot of good things said about him. He is really the anointed man of God. He has delivered many people troubled by spiritual issues. If the deliverance doesn’t work, then you may see a doctor.”

I was silent as I mulled over VaMunyoro’s suggestion. Finally, I said, “Alright, I will go and see Pastor Gumbo if that will stop the lies spreading throughout the village.”

Pastor Gumbo, Senior Pastor of the Anointed Generation Pentecostal Ministries, was a lanky man who wore an expensive black designer suit. He seemed full of himself. He claimed to heal people inside his large, newly built church.

The day I entered Pastor Gumbo’s church, I was paralysed by fear and wondered what was going to happen to me.

A church attendant led me to the front row seats of the church.

“Welcome to the place of deliverance,” Pastor Gumbo began, peering down at me and the other fifty people sitting in the pews. “Today, you will receive your healing through the power in the name of Jesus.”

I decided I did not like him. I remained silent.

Pastor Gumbo’s loud, authoritative voice boomed from the speakers on the podium. “Jesus Christ, the lamb of God, casts out evil spirits. Today, I will preach how Jesus cast out evil spirits from afflicted people.”

“Tell it to us, Papa!” someone in the congregation shouted.

The sermon was long, winding and boring. My belly rumbled. I shifted in the seat.

After the sermon there was joyous singing. Then the church attendants told me and the other congregants in the front row seats to stand up and form a queue, facing Pastor Gumbo on the podium. My knees trembled as I took my place in line. A feeling of fear and emptiness tugged at my belly.

Pastor Gumbo jumped up and down on the podium. He lay his hand on the boy in front of the queue. "Son, I release you in the name of Jesus."

Suddenly, the boy jumped and screamed as if he had been touched by hot iron. Pastor Gumbo charged at the boy and pushed him to the ground. He fell backwards with a thud.

"Be released, be delivered in the name of Jesus." Pastor Gumbo knelt over the boy and shook his head. "Receive deliverance, in the name of Jesus."

"Praise the Lord for deliverance," the congregation chanted.

My stomach tightened. I felt dizzy but steadied myself.

Pastor Gumbo dug his hands into the boy's belly. He massaged it then slapped him on the face. "Son, I order you, in the name of Jesus, to vomit the devil inside you!"

The boy screamed and vomited onto the floor.

I instinctively wanted to puke.

The congregation shouted, "Praise the Lord! Praise the Lord!"

My intestines twisted.

The boy lay prostrate on the floor, barely conscious.

Pastor Gumbo moved on to the young girl who was next in line. He touched the girl on the head and pushed her. She fell backwards, writhing and hissing on the floor. He poured anointed water over her.

The young girl started screaming hysterically.

I could not stand it any longer. "Can I use the toilet?" I asked one of the church attendants.

"Go but be quick. Pastor Gumbo will pray for you shortly," he said before he led me to the women's toilets.

I shut the door behind me. I glanced at the open window. I tiptoed to the window. I heaved myself through the window and landed outside. Adrenalin pumped through my veins. I got up quickly and bolted towards the main gate.

The church attendant saw me. "Hey, you! Stop!" he shouted, chasing after me like a greyhound hot on the heels of a rabbit. He pounced on me before I crossed the threshold of the main gate. "Where do you think you are going?" the church attendant asked, breathing heavily while he pinned me to the ground. He yanked me up.

"Please, let me go. I don't want to go back in there," I cried, trying to free myself.

"You are not going anywhere until Pastor Gumbo has prayed for you."

"Please let me go!" I pleaded with him. The church attendant dragged me by the scruff of the neck back into the church. By the time we got in, I was badly bruised and covered in dust.

Pastor Gumbo glared at me as the church attendant narrated how I had attempted to escape. "The devil had possessed you, child. So, you attempted to escape," he said, looking into my eyes. "What is your name?"

"Vongai."

"Today, the Lord Jesus will deliver you from the powers of the devil." He paraded me in front of the congregation.

"Deliver her, Papa! Deliver her, Man of God!" the congregation egged him on.

I was dying with fear.

Pastor Gumbo laid his hand on my head. "I cast out the devil inside you, Vongai, in the name of Jesus. Vomit out the devil inside you." He spoke in tongues and shook my head violently.

My head was splitting with pain. He pushed me to the floor and I fell backwards.

Suddenly, I felt something snap. I could not feel my arm. "Please stop!" I begged.

But Pastor Gumbo knelt over me and shook my head. He continued praying in tongues. He pressed his fist hard on my stomach.

I tried to stand up, but I fell backwards. Suddenly, I felt faint and collapsed. There was darkness.

***

When I woke up, I lay in a bed inside a room with bright lights. A woman in a white uniform stood over me.

"You are in hospital now and I am a nurse," the woman said. "A man and a woman from Anointed Generation Pentecostal Ministries church brought you here. You fractured your arm and fainted."

Tears glistened in my eyes and poured down my cheeks. There was throbbing pain in my arm.

"What happened at the church? How did you fracture your arm?" the nurse asked, looking directly into my eyes. I started sobbing. The nurse was silent. She drew closer to me.

After a while the nurse said, "I don't believe what one of the church assistants said happened to you at the church. He said you collapsed by yourself. Tell me the truth, child, is that how you fractured your arm?" She read my eyes. I opened my mouth.

Suddenly one of the church assistants walked into the ward. My heart leapt out of my rib cage. I was mute.

The church assistant scowled at me. "What did she tell you?" he asked the nurse.

"Nothing." The nurse looked at me and then at the church attendant. "Please leave the room. I want to examine Vongai in private."

The church assistant hesitated then paced out of the ward.

"Now, tell me the truth. What really happened at the church? You are safe here." The nurse was insistent.

I took a deep breath. "I broke my arm when Pastor Gumbo pushed me to the floor in the church. He was casting out the devil inside me."

"Hmm. The devil inside you?"

"Yes." The nurse shook her head. "And the bruises?"

"I tried to escape from the deliverance service, but I was caught by a church attendant who wrestled me to the ground." Tears sparkled in the nurse's eyes.

I told her everything, about the lies that I was a child witch and how I had been taken to Pastor Gumbo's church for deliverance.

"I will alert the police and the hospital social workers. You must be protected from this abuse from now onwards," said the nurse, struggling to hold back tears. They flowed down her face. She stroked my cheeks.

A heavy weight lifted off my chest. It had been long since someone had listened to me, let alone stroked my cheeks. I felt free.

***

My life has changed since then. The tablets from the hospital have helped me. I feel calm at night and sleep better. I have stopped wetting the bed. I feel happier every day.

A counsellor called Harrison visits me and other children at the school every Wednesday afternoon. He works for Save the Children. He drives a 4x4 vehicle with the words, **Save the Children**, written in bold on the right side.

I always look forward to Harrison's visits. He is a good storyteller. He begins the counselling meetings by telling us funny stories of Hare and Baboon. I laugh and giggle when Harrison speaks like Hare and Baboon.

After that, I read what I would have written in my diary during the week. Harrison gave me the diary. I write down everything - what I have done or not done, what I have dreamt, what I think and feel.

Harrison always listens to me when I read from my diary. "Well done, Vongai," he always says. He does not judge me. He has advised me on how to cope with my mother's death and other problems in my life. He gives me presents from Save the Children such as books to read.

After I told Harrison about the child-witch lies, he went to speak to my grandmother, to Pastor Gumbo, my teachers, and the community leaders in my village. I do not know what was said, but things have suddenly changed. People now respect me in the village. Pastor Gumbo paid my hospital fees. I never returned to his church. Harrison tells me that the police warned him about his deliverance services.

At home, VaMunyoro stopped gossiping behind my back with the other village women. She is now more kind to me. She also listens to me now.

At school, the teachers are now showing more concern about my wellbeing. They ask me how I am. I tell them how I feel, and they support me. I now play well with the other school children in the playground. The headteacher threatened to punish any school bullies calling me names.

I am no longer scared of going to the village borehole. The two women have stopped spreading lies about me. "Good morning, Vongai," they say, smiling, when I meet them at the borehole. I always greet them back politely.

One day I asked my grandmother why the two gossiping women had stopped spreading lies about me.

"When you were in hospital, the villagers convened a meeting and threatened to expel them from the village. The women pleaded for forgiveness and the right to remain in the village. In the end, the village headman fined them two chickens each and ordered them to immediately desist from spreading lies."

"I see." I was relieved.

Although I am trying to forget what happened to me in the village, it hasn't been easy. There is an old Shona proverb that says, *'An axe forgets that it hacked into a tree, but the tree remembers the blows of the axe and has deep scars to show.'* I guess I am like the tree, full of deep scars. Lately, I have been wondering what happens to the scars of a tree. Do the scars of a tree heal, or do they rot and cause the tree to wilt? I want my scars to heal. But only time will tell.

One-Way Ticket Out of Hell

Jenny was sitting on the sofa in the lounge, watching the morning news bulletin on television when the phone rang. She got up and picked up the receiver.

"Hello, I am Penny, a nurse from St Giles Rehabilitation Centre," a soft, female voice said. "I was given your number by Chris' parents. I am sorry to inform you that Chris was seriously wounded in the leg when the army vehicle he was driving ran over a landmine during a patrol."

"Oh, God!" Jenny dropped the receiver. She held her chest and gasped for breath. Her blood pressure shot up.

"Hello… Hello…"

Jenny picked up the receiver again. "Sorry, I panicked and dropped the receiver," Jenny muttered in a frenzy of shock.

"I am sorry to be the bearer of this sad news."

"Oh, God! Can I come and see Chris right now?"

"Yes, you can."

"I'm on my way."

Jenny's hands trembled as she put down the receiver. Tears glistened in her eyes and slowly trickled down the contours of her cheeks. She wiped away the tears with the back of her hand.

Although phone calls bearing sad news were something women with partners serving in the Rhodesian army expected at some point, Jenny had never thought she would receive such news herself. She was shell-shocked and feared the worst for her boyfriend.

In a daze, Jenny jumped into her yellow Datsun and drove slowly through the congested avenues of Salisbury to St Giles Rehabilitation Centre. Her mind whizzed back to the night of Chris' deployment to the war front on a second call up.

***

"You shouldn't go back," Jenny had said to Chris, handing him back the call up letter from the Rhodesian army.

"Listen, Jenny. I must go. I must defend my country from those black terrorists."

"What about us? Do you ever think about us, our love, our careers, our future together?"

"Yes, I do. I imagine us married one day, in peace times, the future Mr. and Mrs. Smith. But right now, there is a war, and the Rhodesian army needs me to fight those Afris, communists and terrorists threating our white civilization and prosperity in this country that our white forebears built with their sweat."

"This country belongs to black people too. Their ancestors are buried here."

"No, Rhodesia belongs to white people. We built the towns and the cities in this country, not them."

"Alright, enough of your bigoted history lesson. What if you get wounded on the war front? God forbid, you die on the war front, I don't know what I would do. I would lose my mind. I want us to spend the rest of our lives together."

"I will be fine, Jenny."

"Why don't we leave this war-torn country for London?"

"London?" Chris laughed. "Emigrate to London, England? Do you want me to leave my beautiful, sunny and scenic Rhodesia and flee to cold England? No chance in hell!"

"Don't you wish to study in London and get a good, well-paying job?"

"No, I would rather die here, defending my Rhodesia than flee to London like a coward."

"You wouldn't be a coward, but a realist. In the not-so-distant future, these so-called black terrorists will take over this country because they have the support of the black masses and the neighbouring black countries. Then, you will be forced to flee, fearing retribution for the atrocities you committed."

"Who will look after my parents and their farm if I flee to London? I can neither leave them to die alone here nor leave their farm to be taken over by those terrorists. Besides, I don't trust the British, not after they abandoned us, after UDI."

"Alright, Chris. I just wanted you to think about our future together. I don't want to reach a point where I might reconsider our future together. You know I hate war, period."

"What do you mean by reconsidering our future together? You mean you might end our relationship?"

"Yes, that might be a possibility."

"I see." Chris paused for thought. Suddenly, his face turned pale.

"Godspeed." Jenny smiled and then kissed Chris on the mouth. There was a strong smell of garlic on his breath. She nuzzled Chris on the forehead, cheek, and neck then winked.

Chris rolled his eyes. He lifted Jenny with his strong arms and carried her to the bedroom. He laid her on the bed where he caressed her hair, back, ears and body. They undressed and their bodies and souls tangoed in sync.

***

When Jenny pulled into the St Giles Rehabilitation Centre car park, her eyes were filled with tears. She looked into the rear-view mirror and quickly wiped the tears away. Her eyes were red. She rubbed some Vaseline onto her face before she composed herself and got out of the car. She sniffled as she straightened her red dress.

A short white nurse met Jenny at the reception area and led her through a large, well-lit open plan exercise room full of injured soldiers of all races – blacks, whites and mixed– engaged in physiotherapy sessions. A middle-aged black man who had an arm missing was sitting alone in the corner, crying. A young white man was practising using his prosthetic leg on the exercise bars. In the far corner, a mixed-race man was practising using his prosthetic arm with the help of a physiotherapist.

Jenny suppressed tears as she strolled through the exercise room, behind the nurse, to the far end of the building where Chris' room was. She followed the nurse into the room. Chris was fast asleep on a large bed. His whole face was bandaged. His heavily bandaged left leg was raised by a leg lifter. Jenny was overwhelmed by emotions and stormed out of the room.

The nurse followed her outside. "Are you alright, Jenny?"

"No." Jenny started crying.

The nurse looked at Jenny with sympathetic eyes. "The doctor recommended that Chris be sedated. He is incredibly lucky to be alive. All his colleagues died in the landmine explosion."

Jenny exhaled. "Will he ever walk again?"

"We are not yet sure about that. Chris' leg will require amputation. He will use a wheelchair for the rest of his life."

"Oh, God!" Jenny sniffled.

"His parents were here to see him earlier," said the nurse. "They are devastated."

Jenny wiped away tears with a white handkerchief. A lump formed on her throat.

The nurse escorted her outside to the car park. "Are you able to drive?"

"Yes. Thanks." Jenny opened the door of her car and slumped in the driver's seat. She put her head on the steering wheel and sobbed. After a while, she drove aimlessly around the streets of Salisbury for about an hour.

Eventually, she parked outside an office building in the central business district. She went inside.

"How can I help you today?" asked a short, smiling, middle-aged white woman.

"When is the next available flight to London?"

"This evening."

"Can I have the cheapest one-way ticket?"

"Are you sure you don't want a return ticket instead?"

"No. One-way ticket, please."

"No intention of returning to Rhodesia soon?"

"No intention."

"One-way ticket out of hell. Fleeing the raging war? Fleeing a relationship?"

"Both."

"I have a cheap one-way ticket to London Gatwick tonight at 6pm. Do you want it?"

"Yes. Thank you." Jenny paid for the ticket and left the travel agency office. She sped back to her flat.

***

Inside her flat, Jenny pondered whether she had made a rash decision, buying the one-way ticket to London. She could still change her mind about leaving and phone the travel agency for a refund, but time was ticking. Why was she leaving Chris in his hour of need? She could have stayed longer in Rhodesia and looked after him. It seemed selfish, unkind, thoughtless, and uncaring to leave him now. Yet her heart wanted out. It seemed the right moment for her and the baby growing inside her womb to find freedom from Chris and the endless, bloody war.

Jenny went inside the bathroom and posed in front of the bathroom mirror. She stroked her small, growing bump. She felt guilty for not telling Chris that she was pregnant, and here she was, on the verge of leaving Rhodesia.

She recalled the intimate moments she had shared with Chris. The touches, kisses, embraces and the love making. She recalled holding Chris' hand tight and resting her head on his chest in the cinema on the last two evenings before Chris' deployment for national service, and then his first call up to the Rhodesian army, respectively.

Then, love felt real. But now, it felt surreal. Jenny felt different about Chris. How would she communicate to Chris her epiphany moment? She dressed and packed her suitcases. Then she sat on the kitchen table and started writing a letter to Chris. It read:

Dear Chris,

I am sincerely sorry to learn that you were gravely wounded on patrol in the army. I am writing to inform you that I am leaving Rhodesia, today, 4th September 1979, for London. I bought a one-way ticket to Gatwick airport. I don't intend to return.

It might appear selfish for me to leave you, now, in the state you are in, but I have thought long and hard about you, me, and the future of our relationship.

The raging war has taken its toll on everyone, including us. A lot of innocent blood has been spilled in this bloody, unending bush war between the Rhodesian army and the terrorists. I do not wish to continue to debate the ethics and morality of this war. I hate war, period. I am a pacifist. I am tired of seeing images of dead bodies displayed every day on tv screens and front pages of newspapers.

I had an epiphany when I visited you today at St Giles Rehabilitation Centre and saw you sleeping in bed, wounded and heavily sedated. I realised that I have two choices; to stay in Rhodesia, look after you, marry you and raise a family with you, in this war-torn country; or to leave Rhodesia with the baby I am carrying and start a new life in London. I have chosen the latter because I do not wish to raise my child in a country ravaged by war.

I hope that one day you will understand my choice. I love you, but I am no longer in love with you. I wish you the best of luck for recovery from your injury, and in finding yourself a good wife to take loving care of you.

I will write to you when the baby is born and provide you with updates on our baby.

Best wishes for the future,
Jenny Gordon

Jenny wiped away tears with the back of her hand. She sealed the envelope and put it in her handbag.

That afternoon, Jenny asked the Rixi Taxi driver to stop outside Salisbury Main Post Office. There, she posted the letter to Chris. A weight lifted from her chest. She jumped back into the taxi, heading for Salisbury airport.

That night, inside the Boeing 707, Jenny inhaled and then exhaled as the aeroplane sped on the runway. She sobbed as the plane took off. She was not sure why she was sobbing; whether it was the guilt of abandoning Chris or the sheer relief of leaving a country ravaged by war, where women suffered in silence when their partners were injured or killed in the line of duty.

For a moment, Jenny wondered what life would have been like if she had stayed and married Chris. She could have spent the rest of her life caring for him, raising a family on his parents' farm, surrounded by diligent labourers. Jenny thought that would have been a sad life.

Then she remembered the baby growing inside her womb. The baby would be born in seven months, in a London hospital. The baby was a promise of new hope and joy in the next chapter of her life. But the baby would also be a permanent reminder, a tie that bound her to Chris and war-torn Rhodesia. Jenny smiled when she remembered the apt words of the middle-aged woman at the travel agency, "One-way Ticket out of hell."

About the author

David Chasumba (snr) is a Zimbabwean writer and poet born in Chinhoyi, Zimbabwe. He developed a deep love for African literature in English at Dandawa High School, Karoi, and spent a lot of time reading books in the African Writers Series and Pacesetters. He qualified as Teacher at Chinhoyi Technical Teachers College (now CUT) in 1994 and taught at Mufakose 3 High school, Harare before emigrating to the UK in 2002. David holds an MA degree in Media and Cultural Studies from University of Sussex, and a PGCE and MA in Social Work from Canterbury Christ Church University. He has lectured in Sixth Form Colleges in England. He is a trained Social Worker in England. David is an avid reader of African and African American literature, and he loves to write stories from the Zimbabwean and African perspective. *The Madman on First Street and Other Short Stories* is his debut short story collection.

His short stories, *The Madman on First Street*, *Lazarus Rose from the Dead*, and *Scars of a Tree* have been previously published by Kalahari Review (2021-2022). He also previously published short stories on the Africa Book Club website and in four anthologies- *The Promised Land* in The Bundle of Joy and other stories from Africa by Africa Book Club (2014)- *An Elegy for Aunt Betty* in Momaya Short Story Review: Treasure (2015); and *The man who had the hands of a baboon* in Small Worlds anthology (2014) and *Baptism of Fire* in Reflections anthology (2015), both anthologies by the Brighton University Literature Society respectively. His short story, *Crossing the Rubicon*, was longlisted in the Fish Publishing Short Story Competition in (2013-14). His new poems, *There are still poets* and *Ode to Archbishop Desmond Tutu* were published in Issue 2 of Mosi oa Tunya Review (2021) and Ipikai Poetry Journal (2022) respectively. His older poems were previously published in Zimbabwe, in literary magazines such as Tsotso Magazine, Writers Scroll and in general readership magazines such as Parade, Moto, Mahogany.

David Chasumba lives in Bexhill on sea, East Sussex, UK.